Starting Out
Triathlon

Training for Your First Competition

Ironman Edition

Starting Out

TRIATHLON

Training for Your First Competition

By Paul Huddle and Roch Frey

with Bob Babbitt

Published by Meyer & Meyer Sport

British Library Cataloguing in Publication Data
A catalogue record for this book is available from the British Library

Huddle, Paul and Frey, Roch with Babbitt, Bob:
Starting Out – Triathlon
Training for Your First Competition
Oxford: Meyer & Meyer Sport (UK) Ltd., 2003
ISBN 1-84126-101-7

© 2003 by Meyer & Meyer Sport (UK) Ltd.
Aachen, Adelaide, Auckland, Budapest, Graz, Johannesburg,
Miami, Olten (CH), Oxford, Singapore, Toronto
Member of the World
Sports Publishers' Association (WSPA)
www.w-s-p-a.org
Coverphoto: Bakke-Svensson/World Triathlon Corporation
Printed and bound by: FINIDR, s. r. o.,Český Těšín
ISBN 1-84126-101-7
E-Mail: verlag@m-m-sports.com
www.m-m-sports.com

We'd like to dedicate this book

to those willing to make the commitment

to train and race the triathlon.

Our thanks to

Diane Buchta,

who contributed her Periodization Schedule

for Strength Training

and Beth Hagman

who pulled it all together.

Contents

Foreword

Triathlon.

There is something exciting about the word. There's something even more special about the sport. Watch the Ironman Triathlon World Championship in Hawaii on television, you'll see lone athletes bucking ferocious headwinds for 112 miles and then staggering through sauna-like conditions on the lava fields during the run. Most people think there is no way they could ever do something like that. Heck, most people think there's no way they'd ever even want to try.

But you're not most people. You watch people facing tremendous mental and physical challenges and think, "I wonder if *I* could do that."

You know what? You can — and, if you use this book as your guide, you will.

The toughest part of triathlon is getting out the door. Get out the door and go to the pool. Get out the door and ride your bike or take a spin class. Get out the door and put one foot in front of the other for a run around your local high school track.

To become a basketball or football or baseball player, you need a very specific body type, quick reflexes and phenomenal hand-eye coordination. For triathlon, you only need to 'tri'.

I'm serious about this. If you go to the pool, you will become a better swimmer; if you ride, you will become a better cyclist; and if you run, you will become a better runner. Guaranteed. We all swam, rode and ran as kids. If you played at the beach, had a paper route or played capture the flag at recess, you already have the basics. Add to that perseverance and desire, and you're on your way.

This book is step one to getting you to the finish line of your very first triathlon. It's the first step in changing your whole life in a wonderful way.

Most events are not the Ironman. There are events with a quarter-mile swim, a nine-mile bike ride and a three-mile run. Some are even shorter. Many can be completed in less than an hour. Intimidating? Not really.

I speak often about my first triathlon experience and how that helped me in everything I do every day of my life. There will be moments during your first triathlon where you will be sore and tired and ready to stop. You will doubt your ability to get through the day. But you will get past that. Just when you feel that you can't swim another stroke, the swim will be over. The same thing will happen with both the bike ride and the run. But that last hundred yards to the finish of your race will make any discomfort you might have had seem trivial. There is no better feeling than the finish line high.

The people in the sport of triathlon are the most supportive you will ever meet. When you go to an event, you are not really competing with anyone but yourself. The goal is to get to the finish line. Some people will swim faster, some will ride faster and some will run faster. But the t-shirt you receive at the finish line is the same for the first finisher and the last one. The key is what you take from the event, what you take from the journey.

For the week after your first event, you will be floating on air. Work will seem easier. Your family will be more special. Life will be better. Why? Because you accomplished something you thought you could never do. You took what sounded like an insurmountable challenge and, by breaking it up into bite-size chunks, you succeeded. It's like having a business card in your pocket that lets you know that, whenever things get tough at work or at home or in life, you can deal with it.

Hey, you can deal with anything.

Why? Simple. Because you're a triathlete.

The journey starts now.

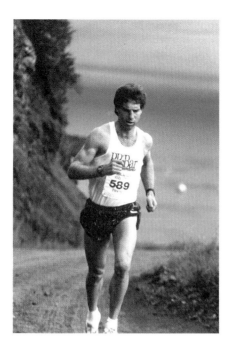

Introduction

by Paul Huddle

Who needs another book on triathlon? Well, **we** do.

Great. That's two people. I'm sure our publisher will be over-joyed at this.

We've finally arrived at that time that comes to every person's life when, theoretically, you've gained enough experience, material, and/or expertise to write a book. That's not to say that you *should* write a book — but simply that you *could*. Such a time has arrived for us. Whether or not it provides you with the information you need remains to be seen. Keep reading.

This book is the result of over 40 (combined) years of training, racing and coaching in the sport of triathlon. Some of those expe-

riences have been successful — others have been dismal failures. Ironically, the failures have been the best teachers and are the basis for much of the material you'll find in the coming pages. What, after all, is the job of a coach if not to help others avoid the same mistakes they've made?

We've had the good fortune to train with, race with and coach some of the best athletes this sport has ever seen. While this experience has been an invaluable part of learning what works and what doesn't work, it has driven home a point that you, the reader, need to always remember when reading a book like this: You are your own best coach.

You're thinking, "So why am I reading this book?" — right?

Hopefully, you're reading this book because you would like to participate in a triathlon and are interested in finding the safest, most efficient and, possibly, the fastest route possible to the finish line. You're looking for some basic guidelines to help you accomplish this goal. This book will provide those guidelines, but we want you to be part of the process.

Realize that, for every champion this sport has produced, there have been as many different training programs. Ask Chris McCormack, Dave Scott, Paula Newby-Fraser, Michellie Jones, Mark Allen, Conrad Stoltz, Erin Baker, Karen Smyers, Greg Welch, Simon Lessing, Heather Fuhr, Lori Bowden, Scott Tinley, Luc Van Lierde, Barb Lindquist, Natascha Badmann, Spencer Smith, Scott Molina, Joanna Zeiger and Loretta Harrop for their training programs, and you'll get 20 different answers. Yes, you'd definitely find some common themes, but the primary reason each of these athletes has had success is that they've been able to adapt the concepts and guidelines that are central to the endurance sport of triathlon to their individual backgrounds, goals and time constraints. This, then, is your job — and it should be considered the key to optimizing your individual potential.

As you follow the program outlined in this book, you'll begin to establish a strength training routine, determine your heart rate zones and plan your week-to-week training. You must incorporate every aspect of what you know about yourself into this process. What is your athletic background? What are your strengths and weaknesses? What is the distance of the event you're preparing for? What is your goal for this event (finish or time)? How many hours a week do you need to devote to work and family — and how much time does this leave for training?

In essence, you should plan your training around your life and not the other way around. Triathlon should be a healthy addition to your life, not an added stress.

While looking at the tangible aspects of your life when executing your training plan, you should learn to trust your intuitive side as well. What does this mean? It means that when you read a passage or suggestion for your training in this book (or any book or article) and it hits you as being exactly what you need in order to improve, trust that feeling.

By the same token, if you read something that you know on a gut level will absolutely, positively not work — trust that instinct. Yes, you'll need to experiment with training intensity, volume, nutrition, etc., but many times you already know what will and what won't work. While experience is the best teacher, learning from the experience of others and applying those lessons individually can get you to your goals much more quickly and with much less grief.

Finally, keep in mind the fact that this is a simple sport. What could be simpler than swimming, cycling and running? These are the same core activities most kids do on afternoons after school and all summer long. Aside from the technical aspects of swimming, proficiency in these three disciplines is primarily dependent on fitness.

If your goal is solely to finish, your fitness level doesn't even need to be particularly high. These aren't terribly difficult skills to master, but they do require a modicum of repetitive practice.

As you sit there right now, we're willing to bet that you could get through a sprint distance triathlon. It might not be pretty. It might take you significantly longer than you'd like — but you would probably finish it.

Take comfort in the knowledge that the first triathletes didn't have coaches, training programs, fluid replacement drinks or energy bars. They had the same desire you probably have to combine three basic modes of human self-propelled transportation in a fun and interesting way. They wanted a fresh challenge, and got it by combining three activities they loved. Through their experiences, we get to enjoy the same healthy lifestyle and satisfaction that comes with training for and completing your first triathlon.

The Golden Rules of Triathlon

Before you move forward, we suggest you consider the following "Golden Rules" of triathlon:

1. Treat triathlon as a sport in and for itself — not a collection of three single sports. Because many first time triathletes come from single sport backgrounds, they try to apply the same training principles from their primary discipline to the other two. If you tried to train each discipline like a single sport athlete, you'd be swimming hard five or six times a week, cycling hard three to four times a week and running hard three to four times a week. This schedule will quickly lead to over-training, injury, illness, joblessness and divorce. When training for triathlon, do only one truly hard workout in each discipline each week. That's right, only one hard workout per sport per week. The core of your training will include five "key" workouts each week: one harder (higher intensity) swim, bike and run workout and one longer ride and run. Everything else should be added and adjusted according to your strengths and weaknesses, goals and time constraints.

2. Plan recovery into your training schedule. It's usually not difficult for most triathletes to do the hard work necessary to complete a triathlon but, once rolling,

it's hard to get them to slow down. All of the hard work in the world is absolutely useless without the recovery necessary to absorb it. If you don't plan recovery into your training schedule, you probably won't get any and your chances of over-training and the problems associated with it will increase exponentially.

3. Gains in athletic performance come from consistent training over a longer period of time. It's not how much you did last week that is important, but how consistently you have trained over a period of months.

4. When it's convenient, don't hesitate to do back-to-back workouts. Too many triathletes try to avoid riding after swimming or running after riding. Since the nature of our sport includes swimming, cycling and running all in succession, doing this in training helps you prepare for these transitions — and it saves on showers! If you're going to run on the same day that you ride, do your run after riding. This tends to be the most difficult of the two transitions. By doing it frequently in training, it will become much easier when you race. The only exception to this is when you are planning to do a hard or long run. These key workouts need to get priority and should be done first.

5. Never do a long and/or hard bike workout on the same day you do a long and/or hard run workout.

For example, do not do your long run on the same day as your high intensity or long bike ride. Since both cycling and running are lower body activities, you'll fatigue these muscles with the first workout and won't be able to get the most out of the second workout. It is okay to do a long or hard swim workout on the same day as a long or hard ride or run, however. Since the primary muscle groups involved in swimming are upper body specific, you won't negatively impact your ability to execute a quality ride or run (and vice versa).

6. Injuries, unfortunately, do occur. If you take time off at the first sign of an injury, the opportunity for quick recovery is best. If you're unsure about a persistent injury or pain, seek out a qualified health professional.

7. Have a plan, but be flexible and learn to trust your own instincts in following the planned schedule. Nothing is etched in stone.

Good luck!

CHAPTER 1

Defining Our Terms

Training programs have their own vocabulary, and our program has some very specific terminology. In order to understand the workout schedule, you'll need to understand this terminology. This chapter spells it out for you.

Throughout this program, we will refer to varying levels of intensity (heart rate zones) with regard to how hard or easy your effort should be in any specific workout. Following is a description of these zones and to what types of workouts they apply.

Target Heart Rate Zones

Level 1 / Easy / HR#1 This could also be called "active rest". This is where you will be in the early season and in between hard workout days during the season. For many people (who, me?), this is the hardest place to be, because they don't feel they're working hard enough. This is the zone, however, where you can maintain your fitness while recovering from harder work.

One of the biggest problems in training is the inability or unwillingness to go easy and allow your body to recover and benefit from the hard work already done.

Level 2 / Medium / HR#2 This could also be called "aerobic endurance". This is a good zone to stay in for your long rides and runs, where the focus is on spending time on your legs, installing the plumbing (circulatory system) and energy systems (mitochondria) that will allow your muscles to work more efficiently.

This is a relatively easy zone to be in, but it requires steady, moderate effort.

Level 3 / Tempo / HR#3 This could also be called "working". Depending on your level of fitness, the frequency and duration spent in this zone will either drop you into an over-training abyss or gradually maximize your athletic potential. As you get fitter, this zone should feel easier and easier. It is not an "easy" level of intensity, but one that you should be able to hold for long periods.

Level 4 / Hard / HR#4 This could also be called the "hammer time" zone. This is where the highest intensity intervals will be done. Like Tempo, however, excessive time spent in this zone will quickly lead to diminishing returns. In this case, abuse does not take long to manifest itself in symptoms of over-training.

Definitions

Anaerobic Threshold (AT) Referred to by some physiologists as the point at which enough anaerobic metabolism occurs so that more lactic acid is produced than can be rapidly cleared from the body. You know this as the point where breathing becomes labored but maintainable. If you continue to increase the pace, you'll soon hit VO_2 max, beyond which you will reach failure (puking and foaming at the mouth). AT is a trainable level. Also referred to as *lactate threshold.*

Maximum Heart Rate (MHR) The highest attainable heart rate. This value is genetically determined. MHR is not a trainable level — it is what it is.

VO_2 Max The maximum amount of oxygen a person can take in and utilize. This level can only be maintained for one or two minutes before you are forced to stop from exhaustion.

Aerobic Literally, "with oxygen". Generally speaking, you're in this range if you can sing your alma mater's fight song or hold a conversation or speak in one word sentences during exercise. As you can see, there is a broad scope of intensities within the definition "aerobic".

Resting Heart Rate Resting heart rate is an easy number to determine. The best time to take it is upon waking in the morning. When you wake up, before you get out of bed, slide your middle and forefinger into the groove on your neck (next to your Adam's apple, if you have one) to feel for your pulse. Grab a watch or look at your clock, relax, and count the number of pulse beats for 15 seconds. Multiply this number by four. That is your RHR in beats per minute or bpm (you can also count the beats for a minute).

Get into the habit of checking your Resting Heart Rate regularly. It will allow you to keep track of your fitness and warn of overtraining and/or impending illness. As you begin to know what your RHR is under normal circumstances, you will recognize when you aren't fully recovered from a workout the day before or might be getting sick. An increase 10% in beats per minute is a warning.

Swimming

Swim workouts are composed of the following three components:

▲ **Warm-up** Easy swimming, getting your muscles and joints loose and ready for the main work set. A variety of strokes, kicking and drills should be performed in every warm-up. Slowly build intensity to prepare your body for the rigors of the main set.

▲ **Main Set** The focus of the workout, this is composed of intervals of varying length and intensity.

▲ **Cool-down** A very important but often overlooked aspect of every workout, the cool-down allows your body to gradually recover from the main set. A proper cool-down helps prevent muscle soreness. As in the warm-up, the cool-down presents another opportunity to enforce correct stroke technique through drills. Proper technique is best enforced at the beginning and end of every workout.

Basic Principles of Swimming

Following are the basic principles that must be properly learned in order to master the freestyle (front crawl) stroke:

Body Position Your body's position in the water is the most

Masters swimming programs are great, but there are no lane lines in the ocean, so get as much practice in open water situations as possible.

Swim Workout Terms

Free   Freestyle or Front crawl.

Stroke Backstroke, Breaststroke or Butterfly.

Kick   Use legs only, with or without a kickboard held in front.

Pull   Arms only, using a foam pull-buoy between the legs to hold the lower body up. Can be done with or without plastic hand paddles for added force and leverage.

IM   Individual Medley. Butterfly, backstroke, breaststroke and freestyle — in that order.

Drill   Each part of the freestyle stroke is broken down into a specific drill to make it easier to learn one basic concept at a time. Examples are: catch-up freestyle, 2 right arm strokes/2 left arm strokes, layout freestyle. Drills are the most valuable tools in helping you swim faster and more efficiently. Swimming is the most technical of the three sports of triathlon. You can have a huge amount of strength, but if it's not applied correctly in the water you may feel like a sinking rock.

important aspect of swimming. Head, hips and heels need to be up close to the surface of the water, allowing you to get streamlined and move through the water like a missile. Kicking drills performed on your front and on your side, both without a kickboard, will help you perfect the proper body position on the water.

You may want to try using a set of fins at first to help you get the feel of your whole body up at the surface of the water.

Lengthening of the body We all know that a longer surf board, ski or boat is faster than a shorter one, so keeping the body as long as possible at all times in the water will ultimately make you a faster swimmer. Rolling from one side to the other while keeping one arm extended in front through most of the stroke does this.

Swimming Terminology

Following is an explanation of the terminology used in the prescribed swim workouts and for swimming in general. All the swim workouts are based on rest intervals within a given set — for example, 10x50 free on 10 sec rest an easy effort. This means, after each 50 freestyle take 10 seconds rest before starting the next 50. You can also perform the set using a timed interval that gives you close to the prescribed amount of rest time: 10x50 free on 1 min. This works best when you've developed a good pace sense, so you know that each 50 takes you about 50 seconds to complete.

Cycling

Like swimming and running, cycling training sessions are broken down based on duration and intensity. The three main training sessions include easy/recovery day, higher intensity day and longer aerobic day.

Easy recovery days The purpose of these rides is to recover and absorb the harder training while maintaining your cycling-specific movements/muscles. While the intensity of these rides might creep up to the middle of HR Zone #2, they should be kept in HR Zone #1. Don't underestimate the extreme importance of these easy rides.

Higher Intensity Days This is your quality ride each week. All quality sessions include a warm-up, a main set and a cool-down. These sessions should be performed at the prescribed intensities (ranging from high HR Zone #2 through HR Zone #4) in order to derive maximum conditioning benefits from your training.

Longer Aerobic Days While the intensity of these sessions could be confused with easy recovery days, the duration is significantly longer. The purpose of this session is geared to the development of the aerobic and fat metabolizing systems. Basically, you are trying to establish the plumbing (capillaries/mitochondria) and cycling-specific joint/muscular strength that will enable you to handle the stresses of the pre-competitive and competitive phases. Upping the intensity of one of these sessions sets you up for injury/burnout.

The Intensity Workout

Sample workout:

▲ **Warm-up:** 15-minute easy spin

▲ **Main Set:** 3x5 minute big gear Intervals at HR#2 as: 2 min in big gear < 80 RPM/1 min in smaller gear > 100 RPM/2 min back in big gear < 80 RPM, 2 min recovery 4x30 sec fast spin, 30 sec recovery

You really need to go to your local bike shop and get set up with a bike and a position that fits you properly. A poor fit leads to back and neck problems – and decreased efficiency.

▲ **Cool-down:** 10-minute easy spin

What that means in English:

After warming up for at least 15 minutes, move right into the Main Set. This entails three, five-minute sets as follows:

After each five-minute effort, you have a two-minute recovery during which you should keep pedaling at a cadence of 80-100 rotations per minute, but at a low enough resistance to allow your heart rate to recover down into HR Zone #1.

"4x30 sec fast spin, 30 sec recovery" means 30 seconds of fast spinning in a smaller gear with low resistance, keeping the RPMs as high as possible while maintaining smooth pedaling (no bouncing butts). The 30-second recovery is back down into a normal RPM of 80–100.

Finish the session with 10 minutes of easy spinning at your own pace.

Big Gear Intervals As the name implies, these intervals are performed in a big gear at lower RPMs than normal. This is like strength training on the bike. It teaches you to efficiently push a bigger gear, developing strength that will help you with time trialing and seated climbing. Stay seated and work the entire circle of the pedal stroke. Experiment with different positions on the saddle. Many cyclists feel they can generate more power when sliding slightly toward the rear of the saddle. Most big gear intervals are performed in high HR Zone #2 to low HR Zone #3 (these are not anaerobic threshold workouts).

Fast Spinning Drills Higher than normal RPM intervals teach your cycling muscles to fire at a higher than normal rate. This will translate into greater economy at your normal cadence and make harder or faster riding less stressful. After performing spinning drills at 120 + RPMs, a cadence of 90–100 feels effortless and makes you efficient at a wider range of pedaling cadences.

Main Set

▲ **2 minutes in a bigger gear (higher resistance)
at a slower leg turnover
(less than 80 rotations per minute),**

followed by

▲ **1 minute in smaller gear (lower resistance)
at a faster leg turnover
(greater than 100 rotations per minute),**

and then

▲ **2 minutes back in a bigger gear
(the same as the first two minutes).**

Throughout the entire five-minute effort, your heart rate should stay in HR Zone #2.

Spinning drills should be performed in your smaller gears with little resistance. Maintaining even pressure on the pedals at higher RPMs and low resistance develops fine neuromuscular motor control. Follow each effort with easy spinning at a comfortable cadence.

Since the goal of these drills is efficiency and economy, you don't need to worry about your heart rate. It may go up briefly but, due to the short duration, the effort will be alactate (very little lactic acid will be produced).

Running

Running workouts during a "typical" training week can be defined as: easy recovery runs, higher intensity days (intervals/track), transition runs, or long aerobic days.

Easy Recovery Runs The purpose of these runs is to recover and absorb the harder training. The intensity should be kept in HR Zone #1. The tendency will be to have the heart rate creep up to the middle of HR Zone #2, but try to stay in HR Zone #1. Don't underestimate the extreme importance of these easy runs.

Higher Intensity Days This is your Key Run each week. All intensity or "Key Runs" are broken up into the following components:

Warm-up An easy jog that allows your muscles and joints to loosen up and be ready for the main work set.

Main Set The focus of the workout is composed of intervals of varying length and intensity.

Cool-down A very important but often overlooked aspect of every workout, the cool-down allows your body to gradually recover from the main set. A proper cool-down helps to prevent muscle soreness.

Transition Runs This is a run performed immediately after

The most difficult part of triathlon is running after getting off the bike. Your legs will feel heavy for the first mile or so. That's the reason we do Transition Runs.

your bike intervals or long ride. You do not need to be in a mad panic to get out the door immediately, just make sure that within 10 minutes of finishing your ride you are on your way. The purpose of these runs is to get your legs used to the sensation of running after biking. The intensity will vary according to how you feel. Some days you will feel great, so roll with it. On the other days, just keep it easy HR#1.

Longer Aerobic Days While the intensity of these sessions could be confused with easy recovery days, the duration is significantly longer. The purpose of this session is to develop the aerobic and fat metabolizing systems.

Basically, you are trying to establish the plumbing (capillaries/mitochondria) and running-specific joint/ muscular strength that will enable you to handle the stresses of the training phases. Upping the intensity in one of these sessions sets you up for injury/burnout.

CHAPTER 2
Strength Training Basics

Strength workouts are as important to your triathlon training as swim, bike and run workouts. This is where you develop your core strength while improving overall fitness and bone strength in a way that sport-specific workouts can't do.

The following is a breakdown of the steps involved in a strength training workout.

Warm-up

Probably the most important part of any workout is the warm-up. What you do in those first ten to fifteen minutes can mean the difference between a great session and a few weeks or months on your butt due to injury. Always, always, always, warm up!!!

What form your warm-up takes isn't as important as making sure your muscles are warm and supple. Ride the stationary bike, get on the stair climber or just walk briskly. It's especially hard when you've already had a big training day, but it's important to get as close to breaking into a sweat as possible before you ask your muscles to lift any weight.

After you've completed a good, general warm-up, we recommend completing the process with the following two exercises:

The Total Body Warm-up

▲ Take a 10 to 25 pound dumbbell.

▲ Stand with your legs shoulder width plus about six inches apart, toes pointing slightly out, holding the dumbbell with both hands.*(Fig. #1)*

▲ Raise the weight from its hanging position below your waistline to above your head until your arms are straight and the dumbbell is directly above you. *(Fig. #2)*

▲ Keeping your elbows in line with your ears, allow the weight to drop slowly behind your head, exactly as in a triceps extension. *(Fig. #3)*

▲ Pause momentarily and smoothly raise the weight back up.

▲ As it goes over your head and then forward past your waist,

Fig. #1   Fig. #2   Fig. #3   Fig. #4

allow your arms to hang straight with the weight. *(Fig. #4)*

▲ Continue through to a squat, but not past 90 degrees with your legs.

▲ Pause, and come back up, repeating the entire motion slowly and smoothly 10 to 12 times.

Robot Arms

▲ Choose 2.5 to 10 pound dumbbells, one for each hand.

▲ Hold arms in a normal run-ning position, elbos locked at 90 degrees or less.

▲ Set one leg forward and one behind in an unexaggerated frozen gait. *(Fig. #1)*

Fig. #1   **Fig. #2**

▲ Swing your arms at slightly faster than a 5K race pace turnover for 50 cycles (50 swings with each arm). *(Fig. #2)*. Remember, the movement is from the shoulders — not the el-bows.

▲ Switch legs and go another 50 cycles.

Although this is a warm-up exercise, it is a great sport specific motion.

The Micro Warm-Up

One last note on warming up: the "micro warm-up" can be used to warm-up a specific joint or muscle group that needs extra warm-up. This simply involves doing a set or two with little or no weight — or with the bar only — prior to beginning the actual set. For example, if you have chronic knee problems or your knees ache frequently, perform a set of 10 reps with no weight before all leg exercises that involve the knee joint.

Weight Training

Most of the exercises should be familiar and simply need to be performed slowly and correctly through the full range of motion. You'll find photos and specific descriptions of key exercises at the end of this chapter. Use a spotter both for safety reasons and to help make sure you're keeping proper form.

The order of exercises is important. Always work the large muscle groups (squats, leg extension and curl, bench press, lat pulldown, etc.) first, then the smaller muscle groups (biceps, triceps, deltoids, etc.). This enables you to work the big muscles without tiring the smaller, secondary stabilizing muscles. It's important to have these stabilizers rested and ready for the heavier loads encountered with the bigger muscle exercises.

Proper technique, speed of execution and breathing are all important. How many times do you see people in a gym benching 200 pounds and bouncing it off their chests? How about those who do their standing biceps curls with a forward bend and subsequent swing back that allows them to handle a much more macho load? These people are more likely to be injured and less likely to get the desired result than those who quietly focus on proper technique.

Number of Repetitions

The number of reps will vary during different phases of your training, but studies indicate that going beyond 8 to 12 repetitions is a waste of time and energy. Current literature suggests that two to three sets of 15 repetitions will maximize your training effort. That's right — more is not better!

Amount of Weight

Generally speaking, heavier weights and fewer reps build power and size, while lighter weights with higher reps emphasizes endurance with minimal gains in bulk. In the endurance phase of your training, your last three reps should feel difficult but not impossible (you should feel fatigued but able to do one more).

The best way to decide how much weight to use in each exercise is to initially estimate the load and then make necessary adjustments as the phase progresses. Begin with a lower weight than your ego thinks is possible for the number of reps indicated. As you progress through the program, additional load increases can be made (but with care!).

You will be given guidelines throughout each phase regarding the optimum level of effort to be exerted within each phase – light, medium or heavy.

Proper Technique

Proper technique means performing each exercise slowly and smoothly through the full range of motion.

▲ **Count one, two on the work (weight raised) phase.**

▲ **Pause briefly at the top (to stop momentum).**

▲ **Count one, two, three, four on the rest (weight lowering) phase.**

▲ **Pause briefly at the bottom (again, to put the brakes on momentum).**

If you use proper technique, you'll probably have to decrease the amount of weight you're accustomed to using, due to the slower speed of execution.

Breathing

The way you breathe during strength training is also important.

▲ **Exhale on the work (weight raised) phase.**

▲ **Inhale on the "rest" (weight lowered) phase.**

Holding your breath is dangerous when lifting weights.

Breathe!

Equipment

Now, what kind of weight training equipment should you be using? There are benefits and drawbacks to both machines and free weights. Much of the decision between the two must depend on individual constraints (injuries, economics, space, etc.) and preferences. When possible, use free weights. They are more realistic in terms of what you deal with in life on a day-to-day basis.

When using free weights, you are required to support the entire load, so the tiny muscles involved in stabilization come into play, not just the muscles that are being targeted. This one factor can provide immeasurable benefits in injury prevention and contribute a core strengthening component that is much less attainable with machines.

The main problem you face with free weights is the very real danger of injury if the exercises are performed incorrectly or with too much weight. Machines offer the advantage of support, safety and the ability to isolate the intended muscle with limited interference or help from other muscles. You can still hurt yourself (you could probably hurt yourself in a padded Volvo), but the risk is much lower.

Machines are best used for leg extensions and curls because they give a constant resistance through the entire range of motion (particularly machines with a cam). Changing the amount of weight used is also much easier.

A combination of free weights and machines is ideal.

Five Phases of Training

Throughout the year, your workouts will be modified according to five phases. These phases are the basis for improvement throughout the year, so pay attention to what phase you are in! Designed by Diane Buchta, they are a great way to get the most out of the weight room, avoiding the inevitable plateaus that come and go.

Your Brain on Weights

The hardest thing about strength training in the early season is that you'll be tired and sluggish in all three sports. You'll put on some extra pounds, but this additional bulk will come off with the sport-specific training you'll be doing later. The gains in injury prevention and performance far outweigh any early season misgivings, however.

On the bright side, the weight you gain comes from increased lean muscle mass and, to a smaller degree, bone density. Keep in

The Five Phases of Training

1. **Base/adaptation phase**
2. **Endurance phase**
3. **Power phase**
4. **Peak conversion/chisel phase**
5. **Maintenance phase**

mind that every pound of muscle gained correlates to a fifty calorie increase in your metabolic requirement. You should expect an increase in appetite, but that's a good thing. If your training levels remain consistent, your body won't allow gain, enough to interfere with running, cycling and swimming. It will adapt, becoming as efficient as possible, to the activities it does from day to day.

When you do back off the gym and head into racing, you will realize the benefits from the work you have put in.

Strength Training Exercises

1. **Warm-up**
2. **Total body warm-up** (see pg 14)
3. **Robot arms** (see pg 15)
4. **Squats / leg press** (see pg 21)
5. **Lat. pulldown** (see pg 21)
6. **Leg extension** (see pg 22)
7. **Bench press** (see pg 22)
8. **Leg curl** (see pg 23)
9. **Dumbbell pullover** (see pg 23)
10. **Walking or reverse lunges**
11. **Seated / Upright rows**
12. **Straight Biceps curls**
13. **Calf raises**
14. **Supinated biceps curls**
15. **Triceps extension**
16. **Anterior tibialis**
17. **Lateral raises (deltoids)**
18. **Standing abduction and adduction**
19. **Back extension** (see pg 24)
20. **Abdominals** (see pg 25)
21. **Press-ups** (see pg 24)
22. **Stretch**

Even if you're short on time, try NOT to miss highlighted exercises.

*Note: If you have any injuries that are aggravated by a particular exercise, don't do it — find a safe alternative. For example, replace the free weight squat with a leg press.

Exercises

Fig. #1   **Fig. #2**

Squats

(Fig. 1) Bar should rest on traps and not on the vertebrae — use towel or pad on bar. Start with upper body straight, lookin forward, legs just past shoulder width apart with toes slightly turned out.

(Fig. 2) Lower to no more than 90 degrees, keeping the knees in line with the ankles.

Fig. #1   **Fig. #2**

Lat Pulldown

(Fig. 1) Arms slightly past shoulder width apart and fully extended.

(Fig. 2) Pull bar down to upper chest with a light lean back from the hips — not neck (so you don't hit your head with the bar).

Fig, #1   Fig, #2

Leg Extensions

(Fig. 1) Start at 90 degrees.

(Fig. 2) Extend legs without hyper-extending at the top. Position bar slightly above ankle joint.

Fig, #1

Bench Press

Arms shoulder width apart. Don't arch your back. Keep feet up on bench to help support your back. Bar should move from mid chest level at the bottom *(Fig. 1)* to chin level at the top *(Fig. 2)*.

Fig, #2

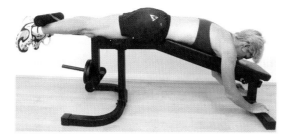

Fig, #1

Leg Curls

Use angled rather than flat bench. Start with knees slightly bent *(Fig. 1)*. Do not lift waist off bench. Use only hamstrings — don't contract lower back or hyper extend neck as you lift *(Fig. 2)*.

Fig, #2

Dumbbell Pull-Overs

Lie on flat bench with knees bent *(Fig. 1)*. Lower dumbbell behind your head to comfortable position, keeping the elbows slightly bent at all times *(Fig. 2)*. Keep your lower back flat on bench throughout the exercise.

Fig, #1

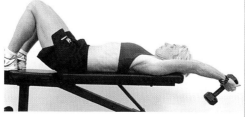

Fig, #2

Fig, #1

Roman Chair Back Extensions

(Fig. 1) Start at less than 90 degree bend at waist in the downward position. Keep back straight at all times.

(Fig. 2) Slowly lift up torso until your body forms a straight line. Do not hyper extend.

Fig, #2

Fig, #1

Press-Ups

(Fig. 1) Lie flat on stomach, palms down, elbows flexed. Move hands forward or backward to maintain hips on floor.

(Fig. 2) Slowly lift up torso until your arms are straight. Do not hyper extend. Keep chin down, looking forward.

Fig, #2

Abdominal Exercises: Crunches

(Fig. 1). Lie on your back, pressing your spine to the mat, knees bent, hands gently supporting the head.

(Fig. 2) Lift shoulder blades upwards, slightly off the ground. Don't pull up with hands on neck. You shold be able to fit an apple between the chin and chest.

Abdominal Exercises: Obliques

(Fig. 1). Lie on your back, pressing your spine to the mat, ankle crossed over knee, hands gently supporting the head.

(Fig. 2) Slowly move right shoulder toward left knee and vice versa. Do not pull up with hand on neck and head.

Fig, #1

Fig, #2

Fig, #1

Fig, #2

CHAPTER 3
Flexibility

Flexibility is an extremely important issue — yet few athletes apply any significant energy toward it. Don't be one of them. While stretching is not the most exciting thing in the world, it is relatively easy to do, requires no special equipment and can be done virtually anywhere. More importantly, it's one of the most important factors in improving and maintaining not just athletic performance but health and well being over the long haul.

Flexibility begins to decrease after the age of 15, but even when it's lost it can be developed at any age. It does not come easily, but is certainly not difficult compared to an interval workout. However, although it doesn't require as much time as our specific sports, stretching does demand focused attention in order to make significant impact.

Improving your flexibility requires patience combined with the ability to remain quiet — both physically and mentally. Flexibility training shouldn't take more than 30 minutes after hard workouts (up to three or four times a week). This time, however, needs to be treated with the same focus as you would give any other workout… it isn't nap time. Remember, skipping this step can lead to injury and burnout. Regular flexibility workouts lead to better recovery — which leads to better quality workouts.

Consistent practice will enable you to identify and troubleshoot potential latent problems. This will happen as you slow down and stretch because of the enhanced awareness of muscles that are being isolated. For example, you'll start to recognize when specific muscles are loose, tight, extra-tight or "on-the-way-to-an-injury" tight.

Basic Principles of Flexibility

1. There must be no contractile force in the muscle being stretched.

Consider the way many people stretch their hamstrings. You bend over while standing and let your upper body hang in space, trying to touch your toes (or knees). If you are standing to begin with, which muscles in your legs are totally relaxed? None. There

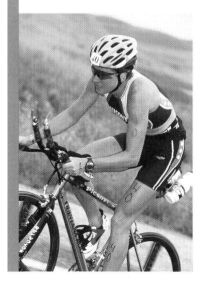

Thirty minutes of stretching after your hard bike workouts will pay dividends when you start doing Transition Runs.

is at least some contractile force in all the muscles of your legs when standing. How, then, can you maximize a hamstring stretch if you're trying to stretch this muscle group from a standing position? Remember rule #1! The solution is to sit or lie down to stretch your hamstrings. This allows your hamstring muscles to fully relax so they can be more effectively stretched.

2. You must isolate the target muscle being stretched.

Slight variations in your alignment (foot, ankle, knee, lower back, shoulder and neck) can help you access specific areas in your body that need attention. Don't push! Go easy and slow, remembering that you just went fast (in your workout) and stretching's purpose is to counter/compensate for that activity. As soon as you isolate the target muscle, breathe and hold. If you push past the initial sensation of tension, you will hinder progress.

3. Breathe with an extended inhale/exhale while stretching.

This alone will aid recovery. Get all that good oxygen into the muscle tissues so they can recover more quickly. Not only does the muscle recover faster with good oxygen transportation, but you also enhance the recovery of your energetic nervous system (kidneys, adrenals, sympathetic nervous system). Finally, smooth, rhythmic, even breathing relaxes.

So you've isolated the target muscle, are sure that it is relaxed and ready to be stretched, and are breathing (duh!) in a smooth, rhythmic manner. Now you're ready to stretch.

There are basically two ways to go about this. Using the hamstring example, find a rope, towel or any other implement with some stretch to it to wrap around your foot. While lying on your back, use the rope to help pull your leg up. The force of pulling on the rope will cause a passive stretch on the targeted hamstring.

If, however, you simultaneously contract the quadriceps of the same leg, you can affect a greater stretch. This is due to a physiological muscular response known as reciprocal inhibition (RI). Simply put, when you contract a muscle (in this case the quads), the opposing muscle (in this case the hamstrings) will relax.

This is known as *active stretching.* You can apply the same principles when stretching other muscles and muscle groups.

The Best Time to Stretch

There's been a lot of debate over when is the best time to stretch. This is one of those questions that is best answered by each individual according to their experience and/or time constraints. Many people find it best to stretch in the afternoon/ evening or within 15 minutes of finishing a workout. Muscles are more pliable when they are warmed up.

For some athletes, it can even be counterproductive to stretch prior to a workout. No matter when you do it, beginning the activity very slowly and increasing pace through out the workout gives the muscles a chance to become thoroughly pliant and receptive to stretching exercises.

The preference for working on flexibility after a workout or at the end of the day when muscles are warmer is supported by studies that have found that the greatest incidence of injury occurs in the morning before the muscles have had adequate time to warm up. If you are a morning person or prefer to stretch before your workout, it is imperative to warm up first. Your body (not to mention your medical insurance) will thank you.

The Stretches

Fig. #1   Fig. #2   Fig. #3

Arm Circles

▲ Begin in a standing position with arms at side *(Fig. #1)*.

▲ From here, swing both arms forward and up *(Fig. #2)* and then continue in this direction until the hands are behind the back *(Fig. #3)* and full circle.

▲ Continue this uninterrupted circular motion 10 to 15 times.

▲ Stop and reverse the direction of movement.

Benefits are best derived if the breath remains smooth, the head and body stay relaxed and the front of the chest remains open. This is a smooth and fluid motion.

Benefits: Arm circles increase circulation and movement of shoulders and mid-back, open and elongate the front of the chest (pectoralis) and generally loosen the shoulder joint. These are especially great after upper body weight workouts, swimming and long hours in a bike position. They are known to aid in prevention of rotator cuff problems.

Triceps Opener

▲ Stand approximately 1 foot away from a wall.

▲ Place right elbow on the wall. The right hand should be placed on or close to the back of the shoulder.

▲ Rotate the left shoulder toward the wall and then begin to gently lean the right armpit toward the wall, keeping the feet and the hips stationary.

Shoulder Opener

▲ Stand sideways with the left hip towards the wall, approximately two to three feet from a wall.

▲ Place left hand on the wall.

▲ Rotate the left elbow forward and then begin to twist the upper torso to the right as the left elbow continues to move forward, creating a stretch in the front of the left shoulder.

Variations can be created by moving the hand up or down along the wall. You can vary the angle at the elbow, but you must rotate the elbow forward BEFORE you rotate the torso back. Common mistakes include rotating the left shoulder in towards the chest and twisting before the elbow is pushed forward.

Benefits: It increases range of movementin the shoulder joint, while releasing and elongating the perpetually-too-tight pectoralis major (front chest muscles). It alleviates rotator cuff problems and excessive interior neck strain.

Shoulder Opener #2 (not shown)

▲ Stand facing the wall (approximately one foot away).

▲ Draw left arm across body.

▲ Place the palm of the left hand on the wall, rotate right shoulder toward the left hand and lean left shoulder in toward the wall.

To obtain a slightly different stretch, place the back of the hand on the wall.

Lunges

Lunges are best done in order and on one side (#1, 2, 3, 4 right leg and then #'s 1, 2, 3, 4 left leg).

Lunge #1

Fig, #1

▲ Begin with right foot back and left foot forward.

▲ Bend the right knee. You should have a sense that the right quad is in front of the right hip.

▲ Your right hand comes onto the back of your right hip and the left hand is on your abdomen.

▲ As you inhale, extend the spine up.

▲ As you exhale, your right hand pushes the right hip forward and the left hand holds your abdomen in.

▲ Continue to rotate the right hip forward until you feel the stretch in the right quad.

Be aware of the tendency to compress the neck and create a sway back (note: this is a bad lunge). A common mistake is to compress the lower back by leaning the upper torso back... And don't forget to breathe!

Lunge #2

▲ Right leg back, left foot forward.

▲ Right knee on the ground/floor (use a towel or pillow as a cushion for the knee).

▲ Strong rotation of the right leg inward, allowing the weight of the hips down.

This is a passive lunge. In this stretch, you may not feel a lot, but you are creating a strong passive opening of the hip joint.

Lunge #3

▲ Left foot is on a chair and right foot is forward.

▲ Begin to rotate the left hip forward (push the left quad forward - similar to Lunge #1), keeping forearms on the right knee.

▲ As you inhale, push left quad forward.

▲ As you exhale, pull the lower abdominals back.

Lunge #4

This is the big payoff!!

▲ Slowly shift the hips back toward the chair.

▲ Continue to slowly rotate the lower abdominals back as you push the left quad forward. There should be a very strong sensation of stretching in the left quad.

Fig, #3   Fig, #4

The lunge set can be very powerful. You should allow time to become proficient at lunges #1 and 2 before moving on to #3 and #4. If there is any discomfort in the knee, bypass this lunge.

Benefits: Lunges help re-establish length in contracted quadriceps and inner thighs (adductors) after demanding workouts. They assist in increasing the circulatory and lymphatic functions of the legs (blood pooling and muscle bloating). Lunges can be an effective means of countering minor cases of patellar tendonitis, strained adductors and illiopsoas problems.

Seated Forward Bend (not shown)

▲ Seated on the edge of a chair, keeping the knees bent, lean the upper torso forward over the thighs, creating a passive stretch of the lower back and spine (erector spinae muscles).

To create more benefits, deeply inhale into the chest and exhale into the lower belly.

Benefits: Like "Standing Forward Bend", this is an extremely beneficial way to release back tension (incurred from sitting for long periods). It's also a great way to take a break at work (but don't let the boss see you).

Standing Forward Bend

▲ Begin by bending your knees and rotating the torso forward over the legs. Bend your knees a lot!! Your abdomen and ribs should come in contact with your quads.

▲ As you get comfortable with the initial position, GRADUALLY straighten the legs.

▲ For each inch that your legs straighten, re-establish contact between the torso and the quads. Relax neck and arms while slowly inhaling and exhaling into the torso.

Common mistakes include: not keeping the thighs and torso in contact, keeping the legs straight and pulling the head back creating compression in the vertebrae of the neck (Bad Standing Forward Bend).

Benefits: The "Standing Forward Bend" helps prevent lower back pulls and strains. In the case of severe lower back pain, start with the "Seated Forward Bend" until pain subsides. Then progress into the "Standing Forward Bend".

Hamstring with a Belt

▲ Lie on your back, right leg on floor, belt (strap, towel, etc.) around the bottom of the left foot (just be-hind the ball of the foot).

▲ Keeping the left leg

straight, raise/lift the left leg to a point where there is a feeling of stretching the back of the left leg. It's more important to keep the leg straight than to lift it high.

▲ Strongly flex the toes of the left foot toward the ground while pushing the left heel up. You get a strong access of your hamstring and your calf muscle.

▲ Breathe. Relax. Recover.

Benefits: In addition to addressing the hamstrings, the two "Hamstring with a Belt" stretches address problems with the calf muscles (gastrocnemius, soleus and achilles tendon). The stretch below also works the iliotibial band and, to a lesser extent, the abductors (muscles of the hip).

Hamstring with a Belt #2

▲ Following the set-up for "Hamstring with Belt", begin to lower the leg that is up across the body (perpendicular to the spine).

▲ Maintain a strong flex in the foot and continue to push through the back of the knee as you rotate the hip away from the ribs while keeping the shoulders flat on the ground. How low should the leg go? Until you begin to feel a stretch in the right hip. DO NOT FORCE THIS STRETCH!! You have an incredible amount of leverage at the hip joint.

▲ Inhale deep into the chest and, as you exhale, pull in the abdomen (as if you were doing a sit-up). This increases the pleasant torsion in the spine.

Pure Hip

▲ Left foot is on a wall, left leg bent to approximately 90 degrees. The right ankle is below left knee, right hand is on the inside of the right knee.

▲ Using the right hand, push the right knee toward the wall. This will activate the stretch in the right hip. Those with tight hips can either start farther away from the wall or move the left foot higher up the wall.

▲ Continue to maintain a steady and relaxed inhale & exhale while elongating the spine and back of the neck. If you have difficulty keeping your head on the floor, support the head/neck with an appropriately sized pillow.

Common mistakes include placing the right shin (instead of the right foot) on the left quad and placing the hand on the top of the knee (instead of the inside of the knee).

Benefits: This stretch directly addresses the gluteals and, to a lesser extent, tensor fasciae, and piriformis. It can also release tension around the sciatic nerve.

Dead Bug

▲ Lie on your back with hips at a variable distance to the wall depending on hip flexibility (the distance can vary from 6 inches – Gumby; to 3 feet – Stiffy).

▲ Place outside edge of feet on the wall. Have the knees and ankles in a straight line.

▲ Position the hands on the inside of knees and push the knees toward the wall, creating an elongation at the inner thighs (adductors).

▲ Continue this set with "Straddle".

Key Flexibility Points

▲ **Warm-up**

▲ **Isolate targeted muscle to be stretched**

▲ **Stretch to the point of light tension**

▲ **Hold (don't go to the point of pain)**

▲ **Breathe**

▲ **Work at this level of tension for 30–60 seconds**

▲ **Follow with a 10–15 second "recovery" (relax the targeted muscle)**

▲ **Repeat each stretch 2–3 times depending on time constraints**

Straddle

▲ From "Dead Bug," push the legs straight out onto the wall.

▲ Slightly rotate the legs in with the back of the knee as close to the wall as possible.

▲ Flex the toes toward the hips and push the heels away from the hips.

This is a passive stretch. Keeping your legs straight is essential; the distance between the two legs is insignificant. Common mistakes in both "Dead Bug" and "Straddle" are hyper-extension of the neck (Sad Straddle). To prevent this, either tuck the chin toward the chest or support the head/neck with an appropriately sized pillow (or towel). Breath is same as "Pure Hip".

To maximize the benefits of lymphatic circulation in the inner thighs, alternate between Dead Bug and Straddle (eg. Dead Bug, Straddle, Dead Bug, Straddle, Dead Bug) – always ending with Dead Bug.

Benefits: The Straddle as been known to greatly enhance lymphatic circulation of lower back and leg muscles (using gravity to aid circulation). This allows you to increase the recovery of the legs while addressing the flexibility of the inner legs (adductors).

Plantar Stretches

▲ Begin standing, hands on the wall.

▲ Slowly walk the hands down the wall, bending the knees (dropping them toward the ground) until a stretch is felt along the bottom of the feet *(Fig. #1)*.

▲ If a stronger access to this area is desired, drop the knees onto the ground and shift the weight of the hips and torso onto the heels *(Fig. #2)*.

Fig, #1

It helps to settle into this stretch. Give it some time. The foot muscles work hard, so they need strong compensation.

If you feel discomfort in the knees, either skip this stretch or place a small towel between your hamstring and calf (back of knee joint).

Benefits: These can help prevent and treat plantar fascitis.

Fig, #2

Improved Flexibility can, among other things:

▲ **decrease the possibility of injury**

▲ **help reduce the soreness that comes with hard training**

▲ **improve joint health by increased blood flow and synovial fluid quantity/quality**

▲ **increase muscular coordination**

▲ **improve kinesthetic sense (your sense of where your body is in space), and**

▲ **reduce stress.**

Fig,
#1

Fig,
#2

Lower Back Elongators

▲ Strarting on the hands and knees, inhale into the chest *(Fig. #1)*.

▲ As you begin your exhale, lower the hips down toward the heels *(Fig. #2)*.

▲ Inhale and lift the torso back to Fig. #1.

▲ Repeat slowly and smoothly for 5 to 10 breaths.

It's important to inhale as you go up and exhale as you go down. This is an active lower back stretch.

Common mistakes are pulling the head back creating compression of the vertebrae of the neck (Don't do this!).

Benefits: These have been known to alleviate an array of lower back problems.

Lat Elongator

▲ From the Lower Back Elongator *(Fig. #2)*, extend the arms in front of the shoulders with the forehead down.

▲ Pause for 8 to 10 breaths, expanding the chest on each inhale and dropping deeper into the position on each exhale *(Fig. #3)*.

▲ Walk both hands to the right while leaving the hips straight.

▲ When maximal lateral stretch is reached (when you can no longer walk your hands to the right), place the right hand on left wrist and lean the left shoulder and ribs to the left *(Fig. #4)*, creating a deeper stretch along the length of the left latisimus dorsi (lat).

To obtain the optimal benefits from this stretch, inhale deeply into the chest and, on the exhale, lean to the left.

Benefits: This enhances the expansion of the rib cage (breathing) and assists with the recovery and resilience of latisimus dorsi (lats — a prime mover for swimming as well as a prime support of one's upper torso on the bike).

Fig. #3

Fig. #4

CHAPTER 4

Weight Training Periodization

A SCHEDULE FOR THE TRIATHLETE

by Diane Buchta, Certified Fitness Specialist

Once you get into the season and the intensity of your sport-specific workouts begins to increase, your weight work will focus more on the upper body. Because of that, your key exercises will change somewhat, and the intensity of others will drop. Keeping a balance in your workouts will help keep you injury-free.

Base Adaptation Phase: 4-6 weeks

Purpose To train the neuromuscular system, to learn the skills and techniques of resistance training and to establish a strength and endurance base.

Speed of Execution All exercises are done slowly through the full range of motion of each muscle group, allowing two seconds to lift and four seconds to lower the weight.

Resistance Light range, starting at 1 set of 10 repetitions (reps) and working towards 3 sets of 15 reps (3 x 15) with light to medium weights. Always think progression… add more weight when the resistance seems easier. Never sacrifice proper execution for more weight.

Endurance Phase: 4-6 weeks

Purpose To increase strength and muscular endurance.

Speed of Execution Slow and controlled, same as adaptation phase.

Resistance Medium range, 2-3 sets of 15 repetitions. You should be fatigued on the last 2-3 reps of each set, but still able to do one more without sacrificing proper technique and speed of execution.

The Power Phase: 4-6 weeks

Purpose To increase strength and power before racing season starts, while increasing muscle hypertrophy and maintaining endurance.

Speed of Execution Explosive yet controlled concentric lifts and slow eccentric lowering. While you still allow two seconds to lift and four seconds to lower weight, you "think" explosive while lifting. Don't jerk, however — keep it controlled. When doing sets of 15, "think" speed, even on endurance exercises. It's actually a matter of learning a mind-set. Control is the important thing. If you can "think" explosive or "think" speed without actually changing the speed of execution, you've got it.

Resistance Some of the large muscle group exercises are done in the medium to heavy intensity range: 2-3 sets of 4-8 reps with weight loads of 85-90% of estimated maximum. Other exercises remain in the endurance phase with medium range resistance, using the same 2-3 sets of 15 reps.

If you are on a 3-day/week (Monday/Wednesday/Friday) strength training program, you will "power" upper body exercises on Monday, lower body exercises on Wednesday and move all ex-

Guidelines to keep in mind during the Power Phase:

▲ Go to fatigue (only go to muscle failure if you have a spotter), but keep proper technique and form!

▲ Increase weights by about 30% on "powered" low rep sets.

▲ Allow 2-4 minutes for recovery between sets that are "powered."

▲ Use a spotter.

▲ On 15-rep or endurance sets, think controlled speed, even between sets. Include faster paced robot arms in warm-up.

▲ Expect to be a little slower and more tired during sport-specific training in this phase. Great results are about to happen!

▲ Eat smart and stay hydrated.

ercises back to the Endurance Phase on Friday. Non-powered exercises will also remain in the endurance phase (2-3 sets of 15 reps).

It follows that if you are on a two-day a week schedule (Monday & Friday) you will "power" upper body exercises on Monday and "power" lower body exercises on Friday. Non-powered exercises (lower body on Monday and upper body on Friday) in the endurance phase (2-3 sets of 15 reps).

Example:

Tuesday

▲ "Power" all upper body exercises.

1. Warm-up
2. Robot Arms
3. Squats/Leg Press
▲ 4. Lat pulldown
5. Leg Extension
▲ 6. Bench Press
7. Leg Curl
8. Dumbbell pullover
9. Walking or Reverse Lunges
10. Seated/Upright Rows
11. Straight Biceps Curls
12. Calf Raises
▲ 13. Supinated Biceps Curls
14. Supine Triceps Press
▲ 15. Triceps w/Strap
16. Anterior Tibialis
17. Lateral Raises (deltoids)
18. Standing Abduction and Adduction
19. Back Extension
20. Abdominals
21. Press-ups
22. Stretch

The Basic Seven Strength Exercises

The Basic Seven don't come into play until the Peak Conversion/Chisel phase, however. They are used through the Peak Conversion and Maintenance Phases. Sports tubing is optional.

1. Lat pulldown

Lunges (optional)

2. Bench press

3. Dumbbell pullover

4. Triceps extensions

5. Supinated biceps curls

6. Abdominals

7. Press-ups

All exercises not "powered" on this day will be trained for endurance, using 2-3 sets of 15 reps.

Thursday

▲ "Power" all lower body exercises.

    1. Warm-up

    2. Robot Arms

▲ 3. Squats/Leg Press

    4. Lat pulldown

▲ 5. Leg Extension

    6. Bench Press

▲ 7. Leg Curl

    8. Dumbbell pullover

    9. Walking or Reverse Lunges

   10. Seated/Upright Rows

11. Straight Biceps Curls
12. Calf Raises
13. Supinated Biceps Curls
14. Supine Triceps Press
15. Triceps w/Strap
16. Anterior Tibialis
17. Lateral Raises (deltoids)
18. Standing Abduction and Adduction
19. Back Extension
20. Abdominals
21. Press-ups
22. Stretch

All exercises not "powered" on this day will be trained for endurance, using 2-3 sets of 15 reps.

The fastest way to the finish line is through the weight room.

Saturday (If lifting 3 days / week):

Bolded exercises (listed above) should be executed to maintain strength using 1-2 sets of 15 reps.

The Peak Conversion Phase
("Chisel" Phase)

Begin approximately 8 weeks before the triathlon season.

Purpose This phase can translate strength into power (or strength applied quickly). Drop all leg exercises except the lunges — save your energy for the miles on the road. At this time, however, you should include speed work in each of your sports. It takes 4-6 weeks for maximum transfer to occur.

Speed of Execution Think SPEED, even in rests. Take 2 seconds to lift, 2 seconds to lower (remember to think control!).

Resistance Do the Basic Seven exercises (see box) in the light to medium range. 2 sets of 10-12 repetitions.

Stop weights entirely 2-4 weeks before important races.

Maintenance Phase

You should be in this phase throughout the racing season.

Purpose To Maintain the strength, endurance, and power gained from the previous phases.

Speed of Execution 2 seconds to lift, 2 seconds to lower.

Resistance Do the Basic Seven (see box) at light intensity 1-2 times/week; 1-2 sets of 10-12 reps.

CHAPTER 5
8-Week
Sprint Distance
Training Schedule

WEEK #1

Spend the first 10-15 minutes of every workout warming up and the last 5-10 minutes of every workout cooling down.

Swim Workouts

Depending on your current swimming ability, adjust these swim workouts by adding or deleting 100-200 yards from all the sets. It's all freestyle unless stated otherwise.

Wednesday Key Swim (1,000 yards)

▲ Warm-up: 200 yards swim

100 yards drill

100yards kick

▲ Main set: 8 to 10 sets of 50 yards each
with 15 seconds rest between each set.

▲ Cool-down: 200 yards easy

Friday (1,000-1,200 yards)

▲ Warm-up: Easy 200 yards swim

▲ Main set: 8 sets of 100 yards each with 15 seconds rest between. Do 2 consecutive sets each of

Freestyle   Kick   Pull   Drill

▲ Cool-down: Easy 200 in your choice of stroke.

Bike Workouts

Tuesday Turbo Workout

▲ Warm-up: 10 minutes spin

▲ Main set: 4 sets of 2 minutes each at a higher cadence. Allow 2 minutes recovery between sets.

Focus on spinning your legs at about 10-15 RPM faster than your normal cadence. It isn't necessary to use a bigger gear — you don't need a lot of resistance. The increase in RPMs will give you the necessary increase in heart rate.

▲Cool-down: 5 minutes spin

Saturday Long Ride

Keep this week's ride between 60-70 minutes. Saturday's ride is designed to build an aerobic base, while keeping the intensity easy (HR#1-2) It is very important to keep this ride aerobic.

Run Workouts

Monday Run

A nice, easy 20-30 minute jog at HR#1 to get things moving. Even on easy days, you need to warm up into the run.

Thursday Key Run

- Warm-up: 10-15 minutes
- Main set: With a stretch of flat road/trail/track in front of you, do 6 to 8 sets of 30-second accelerations.

These are not all-out sprints, just a slight increase over your normal pace, which can be achieved by a faster turnover in your stride. Take a 60-second recovery between each set.

- Cool-down: 10 minutes

Sunday Long Run

Sunday's run is designed to help you build an aerobic base at HR#1-2. It is very important to keep this run aerobic and comfortable. Limit your long run to 40-45 minutes this week.

Abdominals & Stretching

See stretches and explanations in Chapter 3: Flexibility.

WEEK #2

Swim Workouts

Adjust these swim workouts to your current ability by adding or deleting 100-200 yards from all the sets.

Monday (1,000 yards)

- Warm-up: 10x25 freestyle

▲ Main set: 3x200 (200 swim/200 drill/200 pull)

▲ Cool-down: 200 choice

Wednesday Key Swim (1,500 yards)

▲ Warm-up: 4x100 (swim/kick/swim/kick) on 15 seconds rest

▲ Main set: 50/100/150/150/100/50 (1st 50 of each drill, and the rest freestyle) on 15 seconds rest

▲ Pull: 6x50 freestyle on 10seconds rest

▲ Cool-down: 200 choice

Sunday Optional (1,000 yards)

This is just a recovery swim. Swim an easy 500, changing strokes every fifth lap. Then put on your pull gear and pull an easy 300, adding a catch-up drill every fourth lap.

▲ Cool-down: 200 easy

Bike Workouts

Tuesday Turbo Workout

▲ Warm-up: 15 minutes spin

▲ Main set: 3x3 minutes.

Put your bike into a gear that requires you to slow your rpms a little and feel almost as if you were doing a seated climb HR#2. Take 2 minutes recovery between each set.

▲ Cool-down: 10 minute spin

Saturday Long Ride

Keep this week's ride between 70 to 80 minutes. Emphasis is on increasing the duration of the rides, building an aerobic base while keeping the intensity easy (HR#1-2). It is very important to keep this ride aerobic.

Run Workouts

Tuesday Transition Run

Do a 10 minute run at an easy effort of HR#1-2 within 10 minutes after your bike intervals. This is just to start getting your legs used to the sensation of running after a harder ride.

Thursday Key Run

▲ Warm-up: 15 minutes

▲ Main set: 2x30 second accelerations,
              similar to last week's Thursday workout.

Focus on leg turnover, not sprinting. Allow a 60-second recovery. Repeat, except that the accelerations will be 2x1 minute with 2 minutes recovery. Do the pick-up as if you are starting a 10K run.

Finish up with another 2x30 second accelerations at a slightly faster pace than the minute intervals.

▲ Cool-down: 10 minutes

Sunday Long Run (45-50 minutes)

Keeping the emphasis on building a long aerobic base, run at HR#1-2. It is important to keep this run aerobic and comfortable.

Abdominals & Stretching

You will be adding an additional session of abdominals and stretching this week.

WEEK #3

Swim Workouts

Adjust these swim workouts to your current ability by adding or deleting 100-200 yards from all the sets.

Monday (1,500 yards)

▲ Warm-up: 200 free/100 kick/100 free/100 choice

▲ Main set: 4x200 (aerobic interval of 20-25 seconds rest)

▲ Cool-down   8x25 (drill/choice)

Wednesday Key Swim (1,500-2,000 yards)

▲ Warm-up: 6x 100 as: 2 free/ 2 choice/ 2 free
              all on 20 seconds recovery

- ▲ Main set: 16x50 (build in sets of 4, so that the 4th, 8th, 12th and 16th sets are the fastest) on 15 seconds rest
- ▲ Pull: Easy 400
- ▲ Cool-down: 200 choice

Friday Optional (1,000 yards)

It is advisable to include plenty of drills in this optional day of easy swimming.

Bike Workouts

Tuesday Turbo Workout

- ▲ Warm-up: 10 minutes spin
- ▲ Main set: 1x4 minute HR#2, 3-minute recovery
      2x3 minutes, HR#2 high, 2-minute recovery
      3x2 minutes HR#3 low, 3-minute recovery
- ▲ Cool-down: 10 minute spin

Wednesday Optional

45-60 minute easy spin at HR#1-2. This is an optional easy spin after the harder workout the day before.

Saturday Long Ride

75-90 minutes. Emphasis on Saturday rides is to still on increasing duration, building a further base while keeping the intensity easy to moderate (HR#1-2).

Run Workouts

Tuesday Transition Run

10-15 minute run at an easy to moderate effort (HR#1-2) within 10 minutes after your bike intervals.

Thursday Key Run

- ▲ Warm-up: 10-15 minutes
- ▲ Main set: On the road, trail or track you will do 3x4 minute efforts at a pace that is slower than what you perceive your 10K pace to be.

These are longer intervals so go out on the first one easier than you think you should.

Take 3 minutes recovery between each interval, then go right into 4x30 second pick-ups at 10K pace with a minute recovery between each.

▲ Cool-down: Finish up with a nice easy jog.

Saturday Transition Run

15 minute run within 10 minutes after your long bike ride at an easy effort of HR#1-2. Keep this easy, since this is the first week you are doing two transition runs.

Sunday Long Run

50-60 minutes at HR#1-2 — your longest run yet. Emphasis is still on building a long aerobic base. It is very important to keep this run aerobic and comfortable.

Abdominals & Stretching

Same as Week 2.

WEEK #4: RECOVERY WEEK

This is a recovery week, so the intensities will be low and there are no structured intervals for biking and running.

Swim Workouts

Adjust these swim workouts to your current ability by adding or deleting 100-200 yards from all the sets.

Wednesday (1,000-1,500 yards)

▲ Warm-up: 200 choice

▲ Main set: 2x50/1x100 drill
1x100/1x200 pull
2x150/1x300 swim.
All on 15 seconds rest

▲ Cool-down: 4x50 stroke/freestyle
with 10 seconds rest between sets

Friday Optional Swim (1,000 yards)

This is an easy swim with no intervals. Just cruise the full 1,000 yards. Every 4th lap, mix in 25 yards of stroke or drill.

Bike Workouts

Tuesday

Get on your trainer and do an easy 30-minute spin in your small ring. Concentrate on keeping an upbeat turnover.

Friday

Get out and ride as hard or as easy as you feel like for 45 minutes. This ride is mostly just time in the saddle and consistency of training. Extra credit!

Saturday Long Ride

Just a mellow 60 minute ride this week. Enjoy!

Run Workouts

Monday

An optional 20-30 minute jog to start the week.

Thursday

No intervals this week — just cruise for 30-35 minutes on your favorite road/trail at whatever pace feels good.

Sunday Long Run

45 minutes at HR#1-2. Nice and easy!

Abdominals & Stretching

Same as Week 3.

WEEK #5

Swim Workouts

Adjust these swim workouts to your ability by adding or deleting 100-200 yards from all the sets.

Monday (1,500-2,000 yards)

- ▲ Warm-up: 400 choice
- ▲ Main set: 3x (200 swim/100 kick) on 20 sec rest
      20 x 25 (1 drill, 1 easy, 1 build, 1 fast)
      all on 15 sec rest
- ▲ Cool-down: 200 choice

Wednesday Key Swim (2,000 yards)

- ▲ Warm-up: 3x300 as 1 free/1 choice/1 pull
- ▲ Main set: 12 x 75. Descend them 1-4, 5-8, 9-12
      on 20 seconds rest.
- ▲ Cool-down: 300 stroke

Friday Optional (1,000-1,500 yards)

This is an easy recovery swim, focusing on technique and feel for the water.

- ▲ Drill: 1x500
- ▲ Pull: 1x500
- ▲ Swim: 1x500

Bike Workouts

Tuesday Turbo Workout

- ▲ Warm-up: 15 minutes spin
- ▲ Main set: 3x5 minute as 3 minutes in big gear
      and 2 minute higher cadence. 3-minute recovery.
      Descend from HR#2 to HR#3
      4x30 spinouts in a very easy gear with super high
      cadence. 60 seconds recovery
- ▲ Cool-down: 15 minutes

Friday

An easy 45-60 minute, low heart rate spin.

Saturday Long Ride

80-90 minutes. It is very important to keep this ride aerobic.

Run Workouts

Tuesday Transition Run

15-20 minute run at an easy to moderate effort of HR#1-2 within 10 minutes after your bike intervals.

Thursday Key Run

- Warm-up: 10-15 minutes
- Main set: On the road, trail or track,
                  roll into 1x8 minute intervals.

This should start as an extension of your warm-up and build up to what you would perceive half marathon pace to be. In other words, significantly slower than 10K pace.

> Take a 5 minute recovery and roll into 2x4 minute pick-ups at 10K pace with 3 minutes recovery between each.

- Cool-down: 10 minutes

Saturday Transition Run

20 minute run at an easy to moderate effort of HR#1-2 performed within 10 minutes after your long bike ride.

Sunday Long Run

60-70 minute aerobic run. This is the longest run in the eight-week program, so keep it comfortable and conversational.

Abdominals & Stretching

Same as Week 4.

WEEK #6

This is your last "longer" week of training before you begin your two-week taper.

Swim Workouts

Wednesday Key Swim (1,500-2,000 yards)

▲ Warm-up: 2x200 free followed by 8x25 choice
                     with 10 seconds rest between sets.

▲ Main set: 10x100 on 15 second rest intervals.
                     Try to keep an even pace throughout.

▲ Cool-down: 200 easy

Friday Optional (1,000-1,500 yards)

This is an optional swim day.

▲ Warm-up: 200 swim

▲ Main Set: 2x (6 x 50 drill/300 pull) on 10 seconds rest

▲ Cool-down: 100 yards easy

Sunday

Easy 20-30 minute swim of your choice. Best performed later in the day after the run.

Bike Workouts

Tuesday Turbo Workout

▲ Warm-up: 15 minutes spin

▲ Main set: 2x2 minutes, 2x3 minutes, 2x2 minutes,
                     all with 3 minute recovery between each interval.
                     This workout should be done at perceived race
                     effort, HR#3-4

▲ Cool-down: 15 minutes spin

Friday

An optional easy spin. If you are feeling at all tired – skip this!

Saturday Long Ride

80-90 minutes at HR#1-2. This is your last longer ride before you start your taper next week.

Run Workouts

Tuesday Transition Run

20-25 minutes off the bike. Start out comfortably and then let it roll for about 10 minutes at perceived race effort. Give yourself at least 5-10 minutes to jog down.

Thursday Key Run

▲ Warm-up: 10 minutes
▲ Main set: 5x2 minutes at race pace (HR#3-4)
               with 2-minute recovery between each set
▲ Cool-down: 10-15 minutes

Saturday Transition Run

20 minutes at HR#2 within 10 minutes of minutes of getting off your bike.

Sunday Long Run

50-60 minutes at HR#1-2. Start out at a comfortable pace and then let it roll a little toward the end.

Abdominals & Stretching

Same as previous week.

WEEK #7

This is the first week of your taper for the race. While the total duration of your workouts will decrease, the intensity will remain the same.

Swim Workouts

Tuesday (1,000-1,500 yards)

▲ Warm-up: 200 choice
▲ Main Set: 1x300 Swim steady on 20 seconds rest
               6x50 Swim on 15 seconds rest
               8x25 Kick on 10 seconds rest
               6x50 Pull on 10 seconds rest

▲ Cool-down: 4x50 drill

Friday Key Swim (1,500-2,000 yards)

▲ Warm-up: 200 free, 100 kick, 100 drill

▲ Main Set: 3 x (4x50 fast swim on 15 sec rest /
              200 moderate) Take an extra 30 seconds between
              sets and try and make each set faster than the
              previous one

▲ Cool-down: 100 stroke, 300 choice

Bike Workouts

Monday

An easy 45-60 minutes easy HR#1-2 spin.

Thursday Turbo Workout

▲ Warm-up: 10 minutes easy spin

▲ Main Set: 1x5 minutes steady at HR#2
              with 5-minute easy spin recovery
              5x1 minute faster spinning at HR#3
              with 2-minute easy recovery between

▲ Cool-down: 10 minutes spin

Saturday Long Ride

60-75 minutes at HR#2. The length of the long ride has decreased, so pick up the tempo a bit.

Run Workouts

Tuesday Key Run

▲ Warm-up: 10-15 minutes easy

▲ Main Set: 5x1 minute at HR#3
              with 2-minute recovery between. This should be
              slightly faster than race pace.

▲ Cool-down: 10 minutes easy.

Saturday Transition Run

15 minutes at HR#2 within 10 minutes of getting off your bike.

Sunday Long Run

40-50 minutes at HR#2. The length of the long run has decreased, so pick up the tempo a bit.

Abdominals and Stretching

Cut back the abdominal exercises and stretching to one time this week.

WEEK #8

This week, you continue your taper leading into the race on Sunday.

Swim Workouts

Monday (1,000 yards)

Easy, "feel good" swim consisting of 300 swim/300 pull/ 300 drill/100 choice.

Thursday Key Swim (1,000-1,200 yards)

▲ Warm-up: 200-300 yards choice
▲ Main Set: 8x50 on 15 seconds rest at faster than race pace
                8x25 on 10 seconds rest – sprint
▲ Cool-down: 100 kick/100 drill/100 choice

Saturday

10-15 minute easy swim to loosen up your muscles and maybe test out your wetsuit.

Bike Workouts

Monday

Just an easy 45-60 minute easy HR#1 spin.

Wednesday Turbo Workout

▲ Warm-up: 10 minutes easy spin

- ▲ Main Set: 5x1 minute fast spin at HR#2-3
  with 2-minute recovery between
- ▲ Cool-down: 15 minutes easy spin

Saturday

Optional 20-30 minutes easy spin to test out your bike. At least ride your bike for a few minutes to make sure that everything is working properly before the race.

Run Workouts

Tuesday Key Run

- ▲ Warm-up: 10 minutes easy
- ▲ Main Set: 5x20 second accelerations
  with 2 minutes easy between
- ▲ Cool-down: 10 minutes easy

Thursday

An easy 20-30 minute feel-good jog at HR#1-2

Saturday

15-20 minute easy run to loosen up your muscles.

Abdominals and Stretching

Keep the stretching easy this week and omit the abdominal work.

Sprint Training Chart

Week #1	SWIM	BIKE	RUN	OTHER
1 Monday			20-30 min HR #1-2	
2 Tuesday		30 min TURBO 4x2 min Int		
3 Wednesday	20-30 min KEY SWIM 800-1,000 yds			Abdominals & Stretching
4 Thursday			30-35 min KEY RUN 8x30 sec Accels	
5 Friday	30 min 1,000-1,200 yds			OPTIONAL DAY OFF
6 Saturday		60-70 min LONG HR#1-2		
7 Sunday			40-45 min LONG HR#1-2	
Weekly Totals 300 min	60 min	100 min	110 min	30 min

Week #2	SWIM	BIKE	RUN	OTHER
8 Monday	30 min 1,000 yds			Abdominals & Stretching
9 Tuesday		40 min TURBO 3x3 min Int	10 min Transition Run HR#1-2	
10 Wednesday	40 min KEY SWIM 1,500 yds			
11 Thursday			40 min KEY RUN 30 sec/1 min Int	
12 Friday	DAY OFF	DAY OFF	DAY OFF	DAY OFF
13 Saturday		70-80 min LONG HR#1-2		Abdominals & Stretching
14 Sunday	OPTIONAL 20 min 800-1,000 yds		45-50 min LONG HR#1-2	
Weekly Totals 370 min	90 min	120 min	100 min	60 min

Sprint Training Chart continued

Week #3	SWIM	BIKE	RUN	OTHER
15 Monday	45 min 1,500 yds			
16 Tuesday		50 min TURBO 4/3/2 min Int	10-15 min Transition Run HR#1-2	
17 Wednesday	45 min KEY SWIM 1,500-2,000 yds	OPTIONAL 45-60 min Spin HR #1		
18 Thursday			45 min KEY RUN 4 min Int	Abdominals & Stretching
19 Friday	OPTIONAL 20 min 1,000 yds			OR DAY OFF
20 Saturday		75-90 min LONG HR#1-2	15 min Transition Run HR#1-2	
21 Sunday			50-60 min LONG HR#1-2	Abdominals & Stretching
Weekly Totals 505 min	110 min	200 min	135 min	60 min

Week #4 RECOVERY	SWIM	BIKE	RUN	OTHER
22 Monday			OPTIONAL 20-30 min jog	OR DAY OFF
23 Tuesday		30 min TURBO High Cad		
24 Wednesday	40 min KEY SWIM 1,000-1,500 yds			Abdominals & Stretching
25 Thursday			30-35 min run as you feel	
26 Friday	OPTIONAL 20-30 min 1,000 yds	45 min Spin HR#1		
27 Saturday		60 min LONG HR#1-2		
28 Sunday			45 min LONG HR#1-2	Abdominals & Stretching
Weekly Totals 375 min	70 min	135 min	110 min	60 min

Sprint Training Chart continued

Week #5	SWIM	BIKE	RUN	OTHER
29 Monday	45 min 1,500-2,000 yds			
30 Tuesday		60 min TURBO 5 min Int	15-20 min Transition Run HR#1-2	
31 Wednesday	45 min KEY SWIM 2,000 yds			Abdominals & Stretching
32 Thursday			50 min KEY RUN 2 min Int	
33 Friday	OPTIONAL 30 min 1,000-1,500 yds	45-60 min Spin HR#1		
34 Saturday		80-90 min LONG HR#1-2	20 min Transition Run HR#1-2	
35 Sunday			60-70 min LONG HR#1-2	Abdominals & Stretching
Weekly Totals 550 min	120 min	210 min	160 min	60 min

Week #6	SWIM	BIKE	RUN	OTHER
36 Monday	DAY OFF	DAY OFF	DAY OFF	DAY OFF
37 Tuesday		60 min TURBO 2/3/2 min Int	20-25 min Transition Run HR#2	
38 Wednesday	45 min KEY SWIM 1,500-2,000 yds			Abdominals & Stretching
39 Thursday			40-45 min KEY RUN 2 min Int	
40 Friday	OPTIONAL 30 min 1,000-1,500 yds	OPTIONAL 45-60 min Spin HR#1		OR DAY OFF
41 Saturday		80-90 min LONG HR#1-2	20 min Transition Run HR#1-2	
42 Sunday	20-30 min Easy 1,000 yds		50-60 min LONG HR#2	Abdominals & Stretching
Weekly Totals 525 min	105 min	210 min	150 min	60 min

Week #7 TAPER	SWIM	BIKE	RUN	OTHER
43 Monday		45-60 min Spin HR#1		
44 Tuesday	30 min 1,000-1,500 yds		35-40 min KEY RUN 1 min Int	
45 Wednesday	DAY OFF	DAY OFF	DAY OFF	DAY OFF
46 Thursday		45 min TURBO 5/1 min Int		Abdominals & Stretching
47 Friday	45 min KEY SWIM 1,500-2,000 yds			
48 Saturday		60-75 min LONG HR#2	15 min Transition Run HR#2	
49 Sunday			40-50 min LONG HR#2	
Weekly Totals 390 min	75 min	180 min	105 min	30 min

Week #8 RACE	SWIM	BIKE	RUN	OTHER
50 Monday	20 min 1,000 yds	45-60 min Spin HR#1		
51 Tuesday			30 min KEY RUN 20 sec Accels	
52 Wednesday		40 min TURBO 1 min Hi Cad		Light Stretching
53 Thursday	30 min 1,000-2,000 yds		20-30 min Easy HR#1-2	
54 Friday	DAY OFF	DAY OFF	DAY OFF	DAY OFF
55 Saturday	10-15 min Loosen Up	OPTIONAL 20-30 min Spin/Test	15-20 min Easy	
56 Sunday	**Race Day!**	**Race Day!**	**Race Day!**	**Race Day!**
Weekly Totals 295 min	65 min	130 min	80 min	20 min

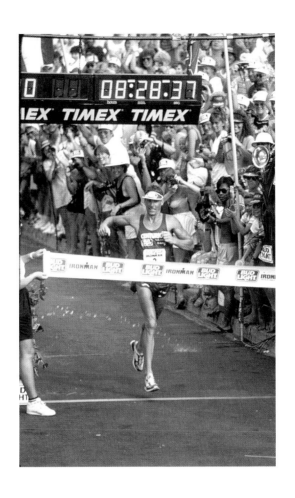

CHAPTER 6
8-Week Olympic Distance Training Schedule

WEEK #1

Swim Workouts

Depending on your swimming ability, add or subtract 100-200 yards from all the sets.

Wednesday Key Swim (1,200-1,500 yards)

▲ Warm-up: 200 swim/ 200 drill /200 kick
▲ Main set: 10x50 on 15 seconds rest
▲ Cool-down: 300 easy

Friday (1,200-1,500 yards)

▲ Warm-up: Easy 200 swim
▲ Main set: 12x100 as: 3x (1 free/1 kick/ 1 pull/1 drill on 15 sec rest)
▲ Cool-down: easy 200 choice

Bike Workouts

Tuesday Turbo Workout

▲ Warm-up: 10 minutes spin
▲ Main set: 6x2 min at a higher cadence, focus on spinning your legs about 10-15 RPM faster. It is not necessary to put it in a bigger gear. The increase in rpms will give you the necessary increase in heart rate. 2 minutes recovery between each set
▲ Cool-down: 5 minutes spin

Saturday Long Ride

75-90 minutes at HR#1-2. Emphasize building an aerobic base while keeping the intensity easy. It is very important to keep this ride aerobic.

Run Workouts

Monday

A nice easy 30-40 min jog at HR#1 to get things moving.

Tuesday Transition Run

15-minute easy run within 10 minutes after your turbo workout. Just get the legs moving and feel easy.

Thursday Key Run

▲ Warm-up: 15 minutes

▲ Main set: With a stretch of flat road/trail/track in front of you, do 6-8x1 minute accelerations. These are not all-out sprints, just a slight increase in pace, which can be achieved by thinking about a faster turnover in your stride. Take a minute recovery between each

▲ Cool-down: 10 minutes

Sunday Long Run

50-60 minutes at HR#1-2. It is very important to keep this run aerobic and comfortable. Emphasis is on building an aerobic base.

Abdominals & Stretching

See the flexibility section for a description of the exercises.

WEEK #2

Swim Workouts

Adjust these workouts by adding or subtracting 100-200 yards from all the sets depending on your ability.

Monday (1,500 yards)

▲ Warm-up: 8x25 freestyle

▲ Main set: 4x300 (300 swim/ 300 drill/ 300 pull/ 300 swim)

▲ Cool-down: 200 choice

Wednesday Key Swim (1,500–1,800 yards)

▲ Warm-up: 4x100 (swim/kick/swim/kick) on 15 sec rest

▲ Main set: 50/100/150/200/150/100/50 (first 50 of each (is drill, and the rest freestyle) on 15 sec rest

▲ Pull: 8x50 freestyle on 10 sec rest

▲ Cool-down: 200 choice

Sunday (1,000 yards)

This is a recovery swim, an easy 500 yards, every fifth lap doing a different stroke. Put on your pull gear and pull an easy 300 yards with every fourth lap doing a catch-up drill.

▲ Cool-down: 200 easy

Bike Workouts

Tuesday Turbo Workout

▲ Warm-up: 15 minute spin

▲ Main set: 5x3 minutes in a bigger gear. Put your bike into a gear that would require you to slow your rpms a little and feel almost as if you were doing a seated climb. Take 2 minutes recovery between each

▲ Cool-down: 10 minutes

Wednesday

Optional easy 45-60 minute spin at HR#1

Saturday Long Ride

90 minutes at HR#1-2. Emphasis is on increasing the duration of the rides, building an aerobic base, while keeping the intensity easy. It is important to keep this ride aerobic.

Run Workouts

Tuesday Transition Run

15 minute run performed within 10 minutes after your bike intervals at an easy effort of HR#1-2, just to start getting your legs used to running after a harder ride.

Thursday Key Run

▲ Warm-up: 15 minutes

▲ Main set: 3x1 minute accelerations, similar to last week. Focus on leg turnover, not sprinting, with a

1-minute recovery. Then repeat, except that the accelerations will be 2x3 minutes with 2 minutes recovery. Have the idea in your mind that you are starting a 10K run when you do the pick-up.
Then finish up with another 3x1 minute accelerations at a slightly faster pace than the 3-minute intervals with 1 minute recovery

△ Cool-down: 10-15 minutes

Saturday Transition Run

20 min run performed within 10 minutes after your long bike ride at an easy effort of HR#1-2. Keep this easy, since this is the first week you are doing two transition runs.

Sunday Long Run

60-70 minutes at HR#1-2. Emphasis is on building an aerobic base. It is important to keep this run aerobic and comfortable.

Abdominals & Stretching

Add a second session of abdominals and stretching this week.

WEEK #3

Swim Workouts

Adjust these workouts by adding or subtracting 100-200 yards from all the sets depending on your ability.

Monday (2,000 yards)

▲ Warm-up: 200 free/100 kick/200 free/100 choice
▲ Main set: 6x200 (aerobic interval of 20 seconds rest)
▲ Cool-down: 8x25 (drill/choice)

Wednesday Key Swim (2,000 yards)

▲ Warm-up: 6x100 as: 2 free/ 2 choice/ 2 free all on 20 sec
▲ Main set: 16x50 (build in sets of 4, so that the 4th, 8th, 12th and 16th ones are fastest) 15 sec rest

▲ Pull: Easy 400

▲ Cool-down: 200 choice

Friday (1,000 yards)

This is a choice day of easy swimming, but include plenty of drills.

Bike Workouts

Tuesday Turbo Workout

▲ Warm-up: 10 minute spin

▲ Main set: 2x4 minute HR#2 (3 minute recovery),

2x3 minutes, HR#2 high (2 min recovery),

3x2 minutes HR#3 low (3 min recovery)

▲ Cool-down: 10 minutes

Wednesday

60 minutes at HR#1-2. This is an optional easy spin after the harder workout the day before.

Saturday Long Ride

80-105 minutes at HR#1-2. Emphasis is to increase the duration, building a further base, while keeping the intensity easy to moderate.

Run Workouts

Tuesday Transition Run

20-minute run performed within 10 minutes after your bike intervals at an easy to moderate effort of HR#1-2.

Thursday Key Run

▲ Warm-up: 10-15 minutes

▲ Main set: On the road, trail or track, you will do 4x4 minutes efforts at a pace that is slower than what you perceive your 10K pace to be. These are longer intervals, so go out on the first one easier than you would imagine. Take 3 minutes recovery

between each interval. Then go right into 4x1
minute pick-ups at 10K pace with a minute
recovery.

▲ Cool-down: 10 minutes easy

Saturday Transition Run

20-minute run performed within 10 minutes after your long
bike ride at an easy effort of HR#1-2.

Sunday Long Run

70- 80 minutes at HR#1-2. With your longest run yet, the emphasis is still on building a long aerobic base. It is very important
to keep this run aerobic, keeping it comfortable.

Abdominals & Stretching

Same as Week #2.

WEEK #4: RECOVERY

This is a recovery week, so the intensities will be low and there
are no structured intervals for biking and running.

Swim Workouts

Adjust these workouts by adding or subtracting 100-200 yards
from all the sets depending on your ability.

Monday (1,500 yards)

▲ Warm-up: 300 choice
▲ Main set: 3x (1x200 swim/15 sec rest
              followed by 4x25 stroke/10 sec rest)
▲ Cool-down: 300 drill

Wednesday (2,000 yards)

▲ Warm-up: 200 choice
▲ Main set: 2x50/1x100 drill
              3x100/1x300 Pull
              4x100/1x400 swim all on 15 seconds rest

▲ Cool-down: 4x50 stroke/free on 10 sec rest

Friday Optional Swim (1,000 yards)

This is an easy swim. There are no intervals. Just cruise the full 1,000 yards. Every fourth lap during the swim, mix in 25 yards of stroke or drill.

Bike Workouts

Tuesday

Just get on your trainer and do an easy 45-minute spin in your small ring. Concentrate on keeping a nice upbeat turnover.

Friday (Optional)

This is just time in the saddle. Get out and ride "as you feel" for 45-60 minutes. This helps the consistency of your training. Extra credit!

Saturday Long Ride

Just a mellow 75 minute ride this week. Enjoy!

Run Workouts

Thursday

There are no intervals this week. Just head out on your favorite road/trail and cruise for 40-45 minutes. An "as you feel" run.

Saturday Transition Run

15 minutes "get your legs under you" easy run off the bike.

Sunday Long Run

60 minutes at HR#1-2, nice and easy!

Abdominals & Stretching

Same as Week #3.

WEEK #5

Swim Workouts

Adjust these workouts by adding or subtracting 100-200 yards from all the sets depending on your ability.

Monday (2,000 yards)
▲ Warm-up: 300 choice
▲ Main set: 3x(200 free/100 kick) on 20 sec rest
                24 x 25 (1 drill, 1 easy, 1 build, 1 fast)
                all on 15 sec rest
▲ Cool-down: 200 choice

Wednesday Key Swim (2,500 yards)
▲ Warm-up: 3x300 as 1 free/1 choice/1 drill
▲ Main set: 12x75, descend them 1-4, 5-8, 9-12 on 20 sec rest
▲ Pull: 4x150 on 15 sec rest
▲ Cool-down: 200 stroke

Sunday Optional (1,000-1,500 yards)
A recovery swim focusing on technique and feel for the water.
▲ Drill   1x500 easy
▲ Pull   1x500 easy
▲ Swim   1x500 easy

Bike Workouts

Tuesday Turbo Workout
▲ Warm-up: 15 minute spin
▲ Main set: 4x5 min as (3 minutes in big gear,
                and 2 min higher cadence), 3 min recovery.
                Descend from HR#2 to HR#3
                4x30 spin outs (very easy gear
                and super high cadence), 1 minute recovery
▲ Cool-down: 10 minutes

Wednesday

An easy 60-70 minutes low HR spin.

Saturday Long Ride

90-120 minutes. It is important to keep this ride aerobic.

Run Workouts

Tuesday Transition Run

20-25 minutes run performed after your bike intervals (within 10 min) at an easy to moderate effort of HR#1-2.

Thursday Key Run

⬚ Warm-up: 15 minutes

⬚ Main set: Once again on the road, trail or track, roll into 1x8 minutes interval. This should start as an extension of your warm-up and build up to what you would perceive half marathon pace to be, in other words, significantly slower than 10K pace. Take 5 minute recovery, and roll into 3x4 minutes pick-ups at 10K pace with 3 minutes recovery between each.

⬚ Cool-down: 10 min

Saturday Transition Run

20 minutes run performed within 10 minutes after your long bike ride at an easy to moderate effort of HR#1-2.

Sunday Long Run

75-90 minutes aerobic. This is the longest run, so keep it comfortable and conversational.

Abdominals & Stretching

Same as Week #4.

WEEK #6

This is your last "longer" week of training before you begin your two-week taper for the race.

Swim Workouts

Wednesday Key Swim (2,500 yards)

▲ Warm-up: 2x200 free and 8x25 choice @10 rest

▲ Main set: 8x100, 4x200, on 15 sec rest,
               trying to keep an even pace throughout.

▲ Cool-down: 300 easy

Friday (1,000-1,500 yards)

This is an easy swim with no intervals.

▲ Drill: 1x500 easy

▲ Pull: 1x500 easy

▲ Swim: 1x500 easy

Sunday

Easy 30-minute swim of your choice. Best performed later in the day after the run.

Bike Workouts

Tuesday Turbo Workout

▲ Warm-up: 15 minutes spin

▲ Main set: 2x2min, 2x3min, 2x2min
               (all with 3-minutes recovery between each
               interval). This workout should be done
               at perceived race effort, HR#3-4

▲ Cool-down: 15 minutes spin

Friday

60-75 minute easy spin at HR#1-2.

Saturday Long Ride

90-120 minutes at HR#2. This is your last longer ride before you start your taper next week.

Run Workouts

Tuesday Transition Run

25-30 minutes off the bike. Start out comfortably and then let it roll for about 10 minutes at perceived race effort. Give yourself at least 5-10 minutes to jog down.

Thursday Key Run

▲ Warm-up: 15 minutes
▲ Main set: 1x5 min, at HR#2, with a 5-minute recovery,
               5x2 minutes at race pace (HR#3-4) ,
               with a 2-minute recovery between each
▲ Cool-down: 15 minutes

Saturday Transition Run

20 minutes at HR#2 performed within 10 minutes of getting off your bike.

Sunday Long Run

75-90 minutes at HR#1-2. Start out this run at a comfortable pace, then let it roll a little toward the end.

Abdominals & Stretching

Same as Week #5.

WEEK #7

This is the first week of your taper. Your total duration of workouts will decrease but the intensity will remain the same.

Swim Workouts

Tuesday (1,500-2,000 yards)

▲ Warm-up: 400 choice
▲ Main Set: Pyramid of 50, 100, 150, 200, 150, 100, 50 all on
              10 sec rest holding steady pace on way up and
              then descend (get faster) on the way down

- ▲ Pull: 10x50 on 10 sec rest
- ▲ Cool-down: 4x50 drill, 100 choice

Friday Key Swim (2,000-2,500 yards)

- ▲ Warm-up: 200 free/100 kick/100 drill
- ▲ Main Set: 2x400 swim at race pace on 20 sec rest; 12x50 faster than race pace on 15 sec rest
- ▲ Kick: 4x25 on 10 sec rest
- ▲ Pull: 8x50 on 10 sec rest
- ▲ Cool-down: 200 choice

Bike Workouts

Monday

An easy 60-75 minutes spin HR#1.

Thursday Turbo Workout

- ▲ Warm-up: 15 minutes easy spin
- ▲ Main Set: 1x10 minutes as: 8 min steady at HR#2, then 1 min big gear, 1 min fast spinning, 5 min easy spin recovery. 5x2 min faster spinning at HR#3 with 2 min easy recovery between
- ▲ Cool-down: 10 minutes spin

Saturday Long Ride

75-90 minutes, at HR#2. The length of the long ride has decreased, so pick up the tempo a bit.

Run Workouts

Tuesday Key Run

- ▲ Warm-up: 15 minutes easy
- ▲ Main Set: 6x2 minutes at HR#3 with 2 minutes recovery between, slightly faster than race pace.
- ▲ Cool-down: 10 minutes easy.

Saturday Transition Run

20 minutes at HR#2 within 10 minutes of getting off your bike.

Sunday Long Run

60-70 minutes at HR#2 — pick up the tempo a bit.

Abdominals and Stretching

Cut back the abdominal exercises and stretching to one time this week.

WEEK #8

You are now in the final stages of your taper leading into the race on Sunday.

Swim Workouts

Monday (1,500-2,000 yards)

- ▲ Warm-up: 200 free/200 drill/100 choice
- ▲ Main Set: 2 x (2x25, 2x50, 2x75, 2x100)
  First time through swim, second time pull,
  all on 10 sec rest
- ▲ Kick: 200
- ▲ Cool-down: 300 choice

Thursday (1,000-1,200 yards)

- ▲ Warm-up: 200-300 choice
- ▲ Main Set: 8x50 on 15 sec rest – faster than race pace.
  8x25 on 10 sec rest – sprint
- ▲ Cool-down: 100 kick/100 drill/100 choice

Saturday

10 min easy loosen swim (test out wetsuit??)

Bike Workouts

Monday

60-75 minutes easy spin at HR#1.

Wednesday Turbo Workout

▲ Warm-up: 10 minutes easy spin

▲ Main Set: 5x1 minute fast spin HR#2-3
                      with 2-minute recovery between

▲ Cool-down: 15 minutes easy spin

Saturday

Optional 20-30 minutes easy spin to test out bike. At least ride your bike for a few minutes to make sure that everything is working before the race.

Run Workouts

Tuesday Key Run

▲ Warm-up: 10 minutes easy

▲ Main Set: 8x20 sec accelerations with 2 minutes easy
                      between

▲ Cool-down: 10 minutes easy

Thursday

Just an easy 30 minute easy feel-good jog

Saturday

15-20 minutes easy loosen-up run

Abdominals and Stretching

Keep the stretching light and omit the abdominal work this week.

Olympic Training Chart

Week #1	SWIM	BIKE	RUN	OTHER
1 Monday			30-40 min HR #1-2	
2 Tuesday		40 min TURBO 6x2 min Int	15 min Transition Run HR#1-2	
3 Wednesday	20-30 min KEY SWIM 1,200-1,500 yds			Abdominals & Stretching
4 Thursday			40 min KEY RUN	
5 Friday	30 min 1,200-1,500 yds			
6 Saturday		75-90 min LONG HR#1-2		
7 Sunday			50-60 min LONG HR#1-2	
Weekly Totals 375 min	60 min	130 min	155 min	30 min

Week #2	SWIM	BIKE	RUN	OTHER
8 Monday	30 min 1,500 yds			Abdominals & Stretching
9 Tuesday		50 min TURBO Big Gear	15 min Transition Run HR#1-2	
10 Wednesday	40 min KEY SWIM 2,000 yds	OPTIONAL 45-60 min HR#1		
11 Thursday			50 min KEY RUN	
12 Friday	DAY OFF	DAY OFF	DAY OFF	DAY OFF
13 Saturday		90 min LONG HR#1-2	15 min Transition Run HR#1-2	Abdominals & Stretching
14 Sunday	20 min Easy 1,000 yds		60-70 min LONG HR#1-2	
Weekly Totals 500 min	90 min	200 min	150 min	60 min

Olympic Training Chart continued

Week #3	SWIM	BIKE	RUN	OTHER
15 Monday	45 min 2,000 yds			
16 Tuesday		60 min TURBO 4/3/2 min Int	20 min Transition Run HR#1-2	
17 Wednesday	45 min KEY SWIM 2,000 yds	OPTIONAL 60 min Spin HR#1		Abdominals & Stretching
18 Thursday			60 min KEY RUN	
19 Friday	OPTIONAL 20 min 1,000 yds			OR DAY OFF
20 Saturday		80-105 min LONG HR#1-2	20 min Transition Run HR#1-2	
21 Sunday			70-80 min LONG HR#1-2	Abdominals & Stretching
Weekly Totals 575 min	110 min	225 min	180 min	60 min

Week #4 RECOVERY	SWIM	BIKE	RUN	OTHER
22 Monday	30 min 1,500 yds			
23 Tuesday		45 min TURBO High rpms		
24 Wednesday	45 min KEY SWIM 2,000 yds			Abdominals & Stretching
25 Thursday			45 min run as you feel	
26 Friday	OPTIONAL 20 min 1,000 yds	OPTIONAL 45-60 min Spin HR#1		OR DAY OFF
27 Saturday		75 min LONG HR#1-2	15 min Transition Run HR#1-2	
28 Sunday			60 min LONG HR#1-2	Abdominals & Stretching
Weekly Totals 455 min	95 min	180 min	120 min	60 min

Olympic Training Chart continued

Week #5	SWIM	BIKE	RUN	OTHER
29 Monday	45 min 2,000 yds			
30 Tuesday		60 min TURBO 5 min Int	20-25 min Transition Run HR#1-2	
31 Wednesday	60 min KEY SWIM 2,500 yds	60-70 min Spin HR#1		Abdominals & Stretching
32 Thursday			60 min KEY RUN	
33 Friday	DAY OFF	DAY OFF	DAY OFF	DAY OFF
34 Saturday		90-120 min LONG HR#1-2	20 min Transition Run HR#1-2	
35 Sunday	OPTIONAL 30 min 1,000-1,500 yds		75-90 min LONG HR#1-2	Abdominals & Stretching
Weekly Totals 640 min	135 min	250 min	195 min	60 min

Week #6	SWIM	BIKE	RUN	OTHER
36 Monday	DAY OFF	DAY OFF	DAY OFF	DAY OFF
37 Tuesday		60 min TURBO 2/3/2 min Int	30 min Transition Run HR#1-2	
38 Wednesday	60 min KEY SWIM 2,500 yds			Abdominals & Stretching
39 Thursday			60 min KEY RUN	
40 Friday	30 min Easy 1,000-1,500 yds	60-75 min Spin HR#1		
41 Saturday		90-120 min LONG HR#1-2	20 min Transition Run HR#1-2	
42 Sunday	20 min Easy 1,000 yds		75-90 min LONG HR#1-2	Abdominals & Stretching
Weekly Totals 625 min	110 min	255 min	200 min	60 min

Olympic Training Chart continued

Week #7 TAPER	SWIM	BIKE	RUN	OTHER
43 Monday		60-75 min Spin HR#1		
44 Tuesday	45 min 1,500-2,000 yds		50 min KEY RUN	
45 Wednesday	DAY OFF	DAY OFF	DAY OFF	DAY OFF
46 Thursday		60 min TURBO 10/2 min Int		Abdominals & Stretching
47 Friday	60 min KEY SWIM 2,000-2,500 yds			
48 Saturday		75-90 min LONG HR#2	20 min Transition Run HR#2	
49 Sunday			60-70 min LONG HR#2	
Weekly Totals 500 min	105 min	225 min	140 min	30 min

Week #8 RACE	SWIM	BIKE	RUN	OTHER
50 Monday	45 min 1,500-2,000 yds	60-75 min Spin HR#1		
51 Tuesday			40 min KEY RUN	
52 Wednesday		40 min TURBO 1 min High rpms		Light Stretching
53 Thursday	30 min 1,000-1,200 yds		30 min Easy HR#1	
54 Friday	DAY OFF	DAY OFF	DAY OFF	DAY OFF
55 Saturday	10-15 min Loosen Up	OPTIONAL 20-30 min Spin/Test	15-20 min Easy	
56 Sunday	**Race Day!**	**Race Day!**	**Race Day!**	**Race Day!**
Weekly Totals 340 min	90 min	145 min	90 min	15 min

CHAPTER 7

Nutrition
and the Triathlete

Before we say anything regarding nutrition, we must give a re-
sounding disclaimer. We're not registered dieticians or doctors and
have no graduate degrees in nutrition. We have had the opportunity to observe and experience the eating habits of some of the
best professional triathletes firsthand, however. In other words,
while some of the ideas and theories we discuss may have actual
scientific merit, others are purely anecdotal. Use or don't use this
information at your own risk.

There, you've been warned.

Some of the best advice we've heard was given to Paul Huddle on his first day of Nutrition 101 at the University of Arizona. The professor wrote three words on the overhead: "Variety and Moderation."

Simple. Perhaps it was too simple. To think that getting by optimally merely required the moderate consumption of a wide variety of foods seems too... simple. We're humans (worse yet, triathletes), and we want to be able to manipulate what we put down our gullets in order to: avoid sickness, improve our complexions, get smarter, steady/alter our moods, lose/gain weight, improve our energy levels, live longer and go faster.

Day-to-Day Nutrition

While we don't want to get into the hornet's nest that is "nutrition" in a general sense, here are some basic guidelines regarding day-to-day nutrition.

Carbohydrates: Current recommendations are 500 to 600 grams (2,000-2,400 calories) of carbohydrate per day for an endurance athlete in order to adequately restore muscular glycogen stores. Of course, this will vary depending on your body weight.

Protein: Current protein recommendations for endurance athletes are 1.4-2 grams of protein per kilogram of body weight per day (or .7 to 1 gram per pound per day).

Fat: While we have not come across any specific amount of fat recommended per body weight per day, current thinking is that the total fat content of your diet shouldn't exceed 30-35% of the total intake.

An additional note on fat: You should understand the difference between "good" and "bad" fats. Try to get the majority of your fat sources from "good" sources: flax-seed oil and olive oil. Studies indicate that Western diets lack Omega-3 and, to a lesser extent, Omega-6 fatty acids. These, besides, being crucial to cell mem-

Food For Thought

Some other ideas we've seen
(some are even documented):

- Prolonged training requires consuming at least 50–60% of caloric intake as carbohydrate (approximately 400-600 grams of carbohydrate daily).

- For rapid muscle glycogen re-synthesis, consume approximately 100 grams of carbohydrate within 30 minutes after exercise followed by additional carbohydrate feedings every two to four hours. A 1:4 ratio of protein to carbohydrate works best.

- Muscle glycogen is maximized by following intense training during the week before competition and then progressively reducing the amount of daily exercise and eating a high carbohydrate diet (approximately 600 grams/day) during the last four days before competition.

- Meals containing 75-100 grams of carbohydrate should be eaten three to six hours before competition to help fill the liver and muscle glycogen stores.

- Carbohydrate feeding of about 24 grams/30 minutes during prolonged strenuous exercise can delay fatigue.

brane repair, have been shown to have an anti-inflammatory effect in muscles & joints (very relevant to endurance athletes). Foods rich in Omega-3 and 6 fatty acids include fish, flax-seeds, flax-seed oil and supplement capsules.

Though it may prove impossible to avoid all bad sources of fat, things to avoid include: saturated fat (fried food & animal fat other than fish), polyunsaturated fat (common in packaged cookies, crackers, margarine, etc.) and any fractionated or hydrogenated or partially hydrogenated fats (look at the label).

For best results, you should consult a registered dietician/nutritionist. A lot of new studies suggest that higher levels of protein and fat than are currently recommended could enhance athletic performance. Sports medicine and sports nutrition disciplines are becoming more refined, and it pays to consult a professional.

Are Vitamins Necessary?

While we go into greater detail on nutritional supplements in the next chapter, it seemed appropriate to address the general topic of vitamins here. Dave Blake from the *Endurance Training Journal* Web page states that:

> "There is significant evidence that endurance athletes undergo greater amounts of oxidative stress than when resting. Supplementation with Vitamins C and E has been shown to reduce this oxidative stress and improve performance. Suggested levels run about 400-800 IU Vitamin E/day and 500 mg to 1,000 mg Vitamin C per day. Always try to take these vitamins with a meal.
>
> Another area that is somewhat neglected for endurance athletes is magnesium deficiency. It has been shown that endurance exercise causes a measurable drop in serum magnesium. Urinary magnesium losses are potentiated by stress caused by exercise, and at

Pre-Race Meals

	SPRINT / 0-1.5 HRS	OLYMPIC / 1.5-4 HRS
Meal Lead Time (Time before Race)	2-4 hrs	2-3 hrs
Calories Consumed (Based on 150lb Male)	200-500	300-600
Intensity	Level #4 RPE = 17+ Very Hard	Level #3-4 RPE = 15-18 Hard to Very Hard

least one study has randomly tested endurance athletes and found close to 50% exhibited signs of magnesium deficiency when tested for urinary retention, which is the best test for deficiency. A deficiency in this mineral will raise blood pressure, magnify the effects of stress and induce insulin resistance, all of which are bad for an endurance athlete. 400 mg/day of Magnesium Citrate has been shown to improve deficiency in athletes.

"As for chromium, its urinary losses parallel the levels of cortisol in the blood, indicating that its losses are stress-induced. Supplementation has been shown to help some people maintain better blood glucose levels at dosages of 200-400 mcg/day of chromium."

Pre-Race Nutrition

Should I eat before a race or not? What should I eat? How much should I eat? Huddle remembers chasing points on the old USTS circuit in 1987–88, waking up in a different city every weekend with an early morning start time and playing the eating game by ear.

Is it possible to eat too much the night before a race?

Yes. If you overeat the night before an event, chances are that you won't sleep well and you'll wake up feeling tired and bloated. Mike Pigg went through a period where he wouldn't eat after 3 p.m. the day before an Olympic distance event because he felt that his body wouldn't be able to derive the most out of that night's sleep.

"If I was hungry and not too nervous, I ate. Other times, I was lucky if I could stomach a swallow of juice. Then came the race in Boston... I woke up at about 4 a.m. to make a 7 a.m. start that was well out of the city center where I was staying. I arrived at the venue about 5:50 and got my transition area organized, warmed up, had a last pit stop in the woods and headed to the water for my swim warm-up.

"At 6:55, they did pro introductions and got us lined up. Then the announcer said, 'Relax, fellas. We need to wait for traffic control on the bike course to give us a go.' We re-staged four or five times after that initial delay and finally got going at about 8:10. By the time I hit the run, I had gone five-and-a-half waking and eleven or twelve total hours without eating a bite. Needless to say, I ran out of gas."

The moral is: count backwards from your estimated start time and make sure you fuel yourself accordingly. Ideally, an athlete can eat between 350 and 700 calories two to three hours before race start time. This might simply consist of a can or two of the Exceed Nutritional Beverage** (now available as Ensure** or Ensure Plus**). Set an alarm for this time, get up, eat, and go back to bed until you have to get up and go to the race.

**Brand is mentioned only for specificity.
We do not advocate one brand over another.

We've seen Mike Pigg down three banana sandwiches on whole wheat bread before races (we almost puked at the sight!). Eat simple food that agrees with you. It may take a little trial and error and some minor burping during the early stages of the race, but the pay-off is not bonking toward the latter stages of an event.

Key Points for PRE-RACE Nutrition

Different individuals will thrive on both liquid and solid forms of pre-race foods. Experiment in training with both forms before your event.

Weather conditions (heat/humidity vs. cold/aridity) will play a huge role in the form and number of calories you can consume and/or keep down (absorb). Once again, experiment before race day, in similar conditions if possible. If that's not practical, experiment during events of lesser importance.

Having your food accessible when you're on the bike is essential. Use your jersey pockets or handlebar bags to hold fruit, energy bars and gel packets. Skip the burgers and fries.

Spread out your pre-race meal. Consume most of your calories early on, but allow yourself to spread the meal over one or two hours. For example, have an English muffin and yogurt first thing, then sip fluid replacement drinks (e.g., Gatorade, Race-Day) in the final half-hour to one hour prior to your start time.

Nutritional Needs During a Race

The factors you need to consider with regard to nutrition during a race are:

▲ Your caloric needs

▲ Distance/intensity of the race

▲ Conditions you expect to face (hot, cool, humid, etc.)

▲ What will be available at the event's aid stations

How do you determine your caloric needs? Can you eat too much during a race? You are limited not by how many calories you burn, but by how much your body can ABSORB. Studies have shown that, during aerobic activity, the maximum number of calories a 150lb male can absorb is in the neighborhood of 250-275 per hour.

During the Race

	SPRINT / 0-1.5 HRS	OLYMPIC / 1.5-4 HRS
Intensity	Level #4 RPE = 17+ Very Hard	Level #3-4 RPE = 15-18 Hard
Type of Calories (liquid vs. solid)	Liquid Water to Light Dilution	Liquid Water to Full Strength* Gel
Calories/Hour	0-100	100-200

*Full Strength refers to "off the shelf" or "mixed per instructions" fluid replacement drink, i.e. Race Day, Gatorade, PowerAde, AllSport, Coke, etc.

Most people try to take in a gel before they get to an aid station so they can wash it down with a cup of water or electrolyte drink.

While there are athletes who believe you can train yourself to absorb more (Mark Allen felt he could handle 400-500 calories per hour), this is a good starting point. If you weigh less than 150 pounds, scale this number back. In training, you should practice getting your calories down while going at distances and intensities that mimic race levels. This, more than any "scientific" numbers, will give you the feedback you need to determine how much you can or can't handle.

Conditions and intensity affect how many calories you will be able to get down and in what form. While we have no scientific research on the topic, it seems that the hotter (and/or more humid) it is, the more difficult it becomes to get calories down and the more dilute/bland the source of those calories should be. By the same token, cooler conditions are usually more conducive to caloric consumption and absorption.

Key Points
for During-Race Nutrition

▲ Different individuals will thrive on both liquid and solid forms of during-race foods. Experiment in training with both forms before your event.

▲ Weather conditions (heat/humidity vs. cold/dry) will play a huge role in what form of and how many calories you can consume and/or keep down (absorb).

▲ Experiment before race day, in similar conditions if possible and, if not, during events of less importance.

▲ Spread your hourly during-race fuelling over 15 to 20 minute increments (don't try to get it all down on the hour!). Because it's typically easier to eat (and absorb) on the bike, try to take in the majority of your calories in the first three-quarters of the bike. For example, if your event calls for 300 calories per hour, try to take in 100 calories every 20 minutes or, better yet, 75 calories every 15 minutes.

▲ If you are going to consume solid foods, get them down early on in the bike leg, where they will likely be more palatable than during the run.

▲ Gels and solid foods (concentrated calories) are best absorbed when combined with water/fluid replacement drink.

If the event is two hours or less, we assume a relatively high level of intensity and corresponding inability to take in significant calories (but, since it's less than two hours, you don't need as many calories, right?). Generally speaking, liquid sources are more readily absorbable than solids. That said, we still suggest practicing with both to determine which works better for you.

During-race nutrition is highly individualized. For example, during a sprint race of an hour or less, Joe Tri-Geek probably wouldn't eat or even drink much of anything (except under the hottest conditions). For Olympic distance races (1.5 km swim/40 km bike/10 km run), Joe should have some kind of fluid replacement drink (Gatorade, Cytomax, Hypocell, Endura, etc.) or water on his bike. Some athletes fill a bottle with Coke (or half Coke/half water) for the extra bit of caffeine and sugar.

On the other hand, when he goes to Ironman Canada, Joe will eat a variety of energy bars in the early stages of the bike and gradually switch to gels and other liquid calories for the remainder of the race.

Practice eating when you train. It's not the most comfortable thing to do but, if your race is going to take more than one-and-a-half to two hours, you won't have enough glycogen (the preferred fuel source for working muscles) on board to carry you to the finish line efficiently.

If possible, find out what fluid replacement drink the event will be supplying — Gatorade, Powerade, RaceDay, whatever — and practice with it.

The last thing to add here is that, nutritionally speaking, what works one weekend might not work on the following weekend. Try to be consistent but, when your old favorite is no longer cutting it, don't be afraid to try something new!

Post-Race Nutrition

Whole books could be written about what and how much you eat after a race, but we're just going to stick to the most important points.

The first order of business after crossing the finish line should be re-hydration. Water and/or fluid replacement fills this need quite well. There is a well-established "carbohydrate window" where your muscles have the best opportunity to refuel optimally. The current recommendation is to consume 100 grams (400 calories) of carbohydrate within the first one-half to two hours immediately following an event/training session.

Simple carbohydrates (e.g., fluid replacement drinks, cookies, fruit) are more easily absorbed than complex carbohydrates. Beyond two hours, the "window of opportunity" diminishes greatly and the chance to become optimally recovered decreases as well.

After two hours or as soon as you're ready to eat, have a well-balanced meal. There should be a balance of protein, fat, and carbohydrate in this meal.

Hydration

A key part of the "nutrition" topic must include what is often even more important than how many calories you get down your throat: Hydration. Though it should go without saying, your hydration status in any endurance event will be a big factor in how well you perform. Studies show that losses of even two to three percent of your total body weight in fluid can result in a significant decrease in performance.

With this in mind, let's consider some basic hydration strategies. Here are some good points on the subject taken from the Gatorade Sports Science Exchange:

When you're racing, your body builds up heat, so it's important to keep your core temperature down by dumping water on your head whenever possible. To get fluid in your body while you're running, squish the cup and tip the drink into your mouth. If you try to drink with an open cup, you'll end up with an electrolyte facial.

▲ Weigh in without clothes before and after exercise, especially during hot weather. For each pound of body weight lost during exercise, drink two cups of fluid.

▲ Drink a re-hydration beverage containing sodium to quickly replenish lost body fluids. The beverage should also contain 6-8% sucrose or glucose.

▲ Drink two-and-one-half cups of fluid two hours before practice or competition.

▲ Drink one-and-one-half cups of fluid 15 minutes before the event.

▲ Drink at least one cup of fluid every 15–20 minutes during training and competition.

▲ Do not restrict fluids before or during an event.

Fluid Replacement Drinks

One point we'd like to harp on a little (especially in relation to longer & hotter events): Don't rely solely on water for hydration. In fact, if possible rely more on fluid replacement drinks (provided they are mixed at a concentration that suits you). People have run into severe problems by taking in too much water in long, hot events (like Ironman races).

You must be conscious of your electrolyte status (the key element being sodium). Depending on who you are, you will lose 1 to 3 grams (1,000-3,000 mg) of sodium per hour in your sweat. On a particularly hot day, this will be a big problem if the event is longer than 4 hours. You can avoid potential problems associated with hyponatremia (low blood sodium levels) by using fluid replacement drinks in addition to water, by lightly salting your food in the week leading up to a long, hot event, and by not overdoing your intake of water.

Some athletes (ourselves included) have used buffered salt tablets by the brand name of ThermoTabs to prevent the problems associated with hyponatremia. Each tablet has 450 mg of sodium. One to two tablets per hour in an extremely hot race that lasts over 4–5 hours taken with water or fluid replacement can be the difference between finishing comfortably or cramping and having to walk the last 10 miles. Buffered salt tablets aren't a magic bullet but are certainly safe and, if you know that you tend toward these kinds of problems, can be a big help. As with anything, try them in training before using them in a race.

Other sources of salt include potato chips (no, we're not kidding) and pretzels.

We're not saying don't hydrate, but you can use a fluid replacement drink to hydrate as well as water. Once you're peeing clear, you're hydrated! This is especially relevant the night before an event. If your urine is clear, quit drinking, get some sleep, and continue re-hydrating when you wake up in the morning.

Additional Reading

Running Research News by Owen Anderson
The Triathlete's Training Bible by Joe Friel
Gatorade Sport Science Institute
Journal of Sports Medicine
The Complete Athlete by John Winterdyk, Ph.D.
The Vegetarian Sports Nutrition Guide by Lisa Dorfman
Nutrition in Sport by Georg Neumann

CHAPTER 8
Nutritional Supplements

Although we don't believe that there is any one thing, nutritionally, that will make you the second coming of Mark Allen or Paula Newby-Fraser, there are some dietary habits and supplements that we do recommend. We'll discuss these as we believe they impact on the performance of an endurance athlete. Some are more applicable to sprint triathletes and others to Ironman distance people.

Please keep in mind that you're an individual. What works for others doesn't necessarily work for you. Consider the fact that the night before the '92 Hawaii Ironman, Paula Newby-Fraser's dinner consisted of 4-5 slices of commercial bacon-cheeseburger pizza, about three leaves of lettuce and about a third of a pan of brownies (slightly undercooked and still warm).* We don't remember what she drank, but she did put milk on her brownies. The next day, she set a course record for women of 8:55.

There you go. There's the magic formula you've been waiting for. "She goes so fast... I wonder what she eats?" Now you don't have to wonder.

Although we weren't there to witness it, we would guess that Mark Allen's pre-race meal that year was much more premeditated and a lot "healthier" — probably including a variety of greens for salad, a protein source such as fish or tofu, some pasta, bread, and fat in the form of olive or flax-seed oil.

Who is right and who is wrong? Take our word for it — there is no right and wrong. There is only what works for you.

Daily Supplements

There are those who insist that, if you eat a "normal, healthy" diet, you will have no problem getting all the nutrients necessary to maintain health and support any extra-curricular, psychotic, over-training activity. We disagree.

Okay, let's take that back. We disagree for the percentage of the population that this book is aimed at —the type A, hard driven, endurance sport aficionado. We also have to wonder who eats a "healthy diet"?

"So, cut to the chase. What vitamins should I be taking?"

The options for supplementation are abundant and constantly growing. You can easily go completely overboard, but that gets expensive — and, according to some people (like your M.D.), it will

Don't try this at home. Remember Paula is a professional.

not do you any good. You could very well end up just paying for expensive urine.

We recommend a multi-vitamin and mineral combination. We'll tell you what we take/have taken, but keep in mind that the brands mentioned are simply examples of supplements or supplement combinations. Other brands are available which contain the same formula(s).

Free Radicals

Perhaps one of the most relevant problems with endurance athletes is that they produce abnormal levels of free radicals. These build up in the body and cause damage at the cellular level. The result is impairment of your overall health and your ability to adequately recover from endurance activity.

Free radical damage can be significantly reduced with the supplementation of anti-oxidants.

It's unreasonable to expect someone to take all of them, how-

Anti-oxidants include:

- ▲ **Vitamin A in the form of beta-carotene**
- ▲ **Vitamin C**
- ▲ **Vitamin E**
- ▲ **Selenium**
- ▲ **Zinc**
- ▲ **Bioflavonoids**
- ▲ **Grape Seed Extract**
- ▲ **Pycogenol**
- ▲ **Alpha Lipoic Acid**

ever, and there are too many possible combinations to discuss here. A common (and safe) regimen might include:

▲ 25,000 IU of Beta-carotene

▲ 500 mg of Vitamin C

▲ 400 IU of Vitamin E

▲ 300 mcg Selenium

Ergogenic Aids

Ergogenic aids include anything that improves or is thought to improve physical performance. This is probably the topic you're most interest in — it's only human to want "something for nothing".

Examples of ergogenic aids include: vitamins, sports drinks, water, carbohydrates (or food of any kind, for that matter), music, hypnosis, disc wheels, titanium, wetsuits... For the purposes of this chapter, though, just assume that we're referring to substances that can be ingested.

Our daily in-season vitamin regimen*

1. 2 SPECTRA* Multivitamin tablets

2. 1 Trader Joe's* Vitamin E capsule (400 I.U.) taken before noon with a meal.

3. 1-3 Trader Joe's 500 mg Vitamin C tablets taken before noon with a meal and sometimes during the course of the day.

4. 1 Trader Joe's anti-oxidant formula tablet

5. 1 Trader Joe's B Vitamin combination.

That's about it for our consistent intake.

*Brand is mentioned only for specificity.
We do not advocate one brand over another.*

Although we certainly do not condone the use of any illegal substance to improve performance, we don't consider a cup of coffee before a race "illegal". There is a variety of nutritional sources that might help you achieve that extra edge, and we don't consider that a problem, either. Still, we're proud of the fact that Triathlon is a clean sport (at least in our experience) and would like it to remain so.

▲ **Adaptogens** These include a wide variety of herbal supplements including (but not limited to): astragalus, echinacea, ginseng (Siberian, Korean, etc.), condonopsitis, licorice root, sarsaparilla, schizandra, ginkgo and wild yam. All of these are purported to assist the body's ability to adapt to physical and chemical stresses. Many are used to control and/or alleviate symptoms of stress.

You must carefully read the labels of adaptogen preparations, because illegal substances (Ma Huang or ephedra, for instance) are commonly included.

Adaptogens can be found over the counter in health food stores, usually in herbal preparations, both liquid & capsule.

▲ **Branch Chain Amino Acids (BCAAs)** Examples include the essential amino acids leucine, isoleucine and valine. BCAAs are thought to enhance performance by, among other things, reducing fatigue during exercise and maintaining overall health during periods of training and recovery. There is research that supports and research that disputes their value for endurance athletes. BCAAs can be found in a variety of supplement forms (tablets, capsules, powders and liquid) and in combination with other supplement formulas/preparations.

▲ **Androstenedione** Androstenedione is an anabolic steroid (and therefore illegal) that is a precursor to testosterone. An athlete might take it for temporarily increased testosterone levels which would enhance their ability to train and race at a higher intensity. Negative side-effects include premature baldness, abnormal breast enlargement in males, aggressive behavior, reduced testicle size, decreased production of sperm and stunted growth, among others. Long-term side-effects? Steroids have been connected to hormone-driven cancers (testicular, breast, prostate, etc.) and heart disease.

Why even mention this if it's so bad? Because it is both extremely popular and dangerous. "Andro" can be found over the counter in health food stores & pharmacies. Please be aware that "over the counter" does not equate to "safe and effective".

▲ **Caffeine** For endurance athletes, perhaps the most popular legal ergogenic aid that we've seen conclusive literature on is caffeine. It extends your ability to work aerobically by releasing free fatty acids and therefore sparing glycogen as an energy source. In addition to this, caffeine has been shown to lower your level of perceived effort and increase the time you're able to spend at sub-maximal levels of intensity. It has been shown to have a much lower diuretic/dehydration effect during exercise than during a sedentary state. However, those who consume caffeine regularly will develop a tolerance and therefore notice less of a positive effect than those who only use it in competition. If you abstain during training and have a cup of coffee the morning of a race, for example, the effects are greater.

Keep in mind that caffeine is a banned substance under USOC and USA Triathlon rules. The levels that would get you disqualified, however, equate to drinking six to eight strong cups of drip coffee within an hour. Even if you don't ever expect to be tested, it has been shown that excessive amounts of caffeine actually hurt endurance performance.

Common sources of caffeine include cola drinks, coffee, tea and tablets.

▲ **Choline** This is a vitamin-like compound which is essential for proper production of acetylcholine by nerve cells. Acetylcholine is a primary neurotransmitter and, therefore, crucial to brain and muscular function. Levels of choline have been shown to decrease after an hour of aerobic activity, which contributes to increased fatigue. Oral supplementation can restore normal levels and have been shown to combat physical and mental weariness. Possible negative side effects include diarrhea and stomach upset.

Common sources include liver, cauliflower, soybeans, spinach, lettuce, nuts, wheat germ, eggs and the drink, Pro-Enhancer.

▲ **Creatine** A combination of amino-acids, creatine is stored in the muscle in the form of creatine phosphate. Used as an energy source during maximal exertion under 15 seconds in duration, this substance is among the hottest selling supplements for athletes from all sports. Although thought to benefit only explosive athletes, creatine has been shown to buffer blood lactate, which allows you to work at higher levels during intense workouts. The end result is an increase in lactate threshold.

Recent studies show that a six-day loading period of six grams per day (when taken with food to slow the absorption rate) is as effective as the previous recommendation of an initial one-week loading period of 20-30 grams a day. The maintenance dosage, after the initial one-week loading period, is two to three grams per day over an 8-12-week period.

Negative side effects include stomach upset/diarrhea, muscle cramping (especially in hot environments) and fluid retention/bloating. Common sources include meats (beef, chicken, fish, etc.) and various supplements (capsules or powders).

▲ **Chromium** An essential trace mineral, Chromium is thought to enhance the action of insulin, although recent studies have shown little if any benefits in endurance performance. Side-effects include anemia, cognitive impairment, chromosome damage and gastrointestinal intolerance.

Sources include mushrooms, prunes, nuts, whole grain breads and cereals and supplementation.

▲ **DHEA** Dehydroepiandrosterone (ouch!), a.k.a. DHEA, got a lot of press in the mid-1990s as the second coming of ingestible substances. It's touted as having the capacity to: burn fat; control weight gain; prevent heart disease, Alzheimer's, breast cancer and osteoporosis (in post-menopausal women); and generally enhance recovery in endurance athletes. So it's not surprising that a lot of people are jumping on the bandwagon. The claims, many actually backed up by studies on rats, rabbits and even the occasional human, have fuelled a fire of positive media exposure. It's readily available in health food stores, but that doesn't make it legal for a competitive athlete. If they find it in your urine, the USOC will ban you for two years from competition.

So what is DHEA? It is an androgenic steroid produced by your adrenal glands as a precursor to a wide variety of hormones, chiefly testosterone.

The following is a sampling from a company that sells it as a supplement:

> **"Referred to by researchers as the mother of all hormones, DHEA is the most common hormone in our body and is a natural steroid that is present in larger amounts in healthy individuals... This wonderful substance is abundant in our bodies when we are about 20 years old but continues to decrease with time. ...Interestingly, the steadily declining levels of DHEA in our bloodstream as we age matches perfectly the increasing incidence of the killer diseases cancer, heart disease (including atherosclerosis) and Alzheimer's."**

Who do I give my money to?!

Dr. Miller goes on to say that supplemental DHEA probably does have some good positive effects for athletes (like enhanced recovery and greater muscle mass), but the fact is that DHEA is a banned substance. Recent positive articles in the lay press has the people at the USOC drug hotline worried that athletes will take the hormone believing all the purported health benefits being written about and then it shows up positive at an event or out-of-competition test. This is not a harmless herbal or vitamin supplement. It is a hormone that has broad effects on the balance of your body's endocrine system. Steroids (and DHEA is a steroid) have been connected to hormone-driven cancers (testicular, breast, prostate, etc.) and heart disease as well as a host of other problems.

In case you missed it the first time, catch it now:

> ## DHEA is an anabolic steroid and is on the USOC and USA Triathlon banned lists.

Glucosamine Sulfate/Chondroitin Sulfate These are nutritional supplements thought to help those with joint problems including osteo-arthritis and general joint achy-ness. While studies support the use of both GS and CS for alleviating symptoms of osteo-arthritis, there have been no conclusive studies on endurance athletes. That said, there are many anecdotal cases (testimonials) supporting these supplements. Common dosage is 400-500 mg three times per day. They are commonly found in the cartilaginous portions of meat and in supplements. No negative side-effects have been reported, but no long-term studies have been conducted, either.

Glutamine In an article published in the February, 1996 issue of Sports Medicine, an Australian study found the amino-acid L-glutamine to be an indicator of exercise stress and over-training. The study, which included triathletes in its test population, was aimed at using levels of glutamine reserves in the muscles and plasma to monitor over-training.

The most abundant amino-acid in human muscle and plasma, glutamine, is essential for the optimal functioning of a number of tissues in the body, particularly the immune system and the gut.

The study found that athletes, suffering from over-training syndrome, appear to maintain low plasma glutamine levels for months or years. Researchers suggested that oral supplementation might be one way to return these levels to normal.

The following out-of-context quotes hit home with us:

"Consequently, decreased plasma levels of glutamine have been suggested to cause impairment of immune function, a compromised ability to respond to immune challenge, and an increased risk of infection.

"Consequently, glutamine may have a role to play at a neural level, by altering perceived exertion, lethargy or energy levels.

"...There is now substantial evidence that food intake can influence plasma glutamine levels.

"After exercise, changes in muscle amino-acid levels showed decreases in only glutamine (19%) and glutamate (39%) levels. All other muscle amino acid levels either increased or did not change after the exercise protocol.

"Decombaz et al. reported that the changes in plasma glutamine levels observed in trained athletes, following a 100 km run, had not returned to pre-exercise values even after 24 hours of recovery.

" ...The lowest levels were observed between four and six hours after exercise...

"In a ten-day period of overload training on the resting plasma glutamine level of elite soldiers, the authors reported a 50% reduction in resting levels by the end of the ten-day study period accompanied by significant reductions in performance in a standardized running test... pre-exercise plasma glutamine levels were not restored until after six days of recovery.

"It has been proposed that decreases in plasma glutamine level could have profound effects on the functioning of the immune system... This may help to explain anecdotal and epidemiological evidence of recurrent infections during periods of over-training and in the over-training syndrome."

So what? Should you go out and buy up a lifetime supply of glutamine? Based on this study (and after consulting with our primary health provider), we would consider taking L-glutamine as an oral supplement. As with any amino-acid, take it on an empty stomach an hour before eating. This gives it the best chance of being absorbed. In its conclusion, the study reported:

"...It has been reported that orally fed glutamine may be a safe and effective means of providing additional free glutamine to the body... It has also been suggested that in conditions where the plasma glutamine level is decreased, exogenous provision of glutamine may be beneficial, particularly to the functioning of the immune system. It is tempting to suggest that oral supplementation of glutamine may be beneficial to athletes during periods of overload training by sparing intra-muscular glutamine, helping to maintain plasma glutamine levels and possibly preventing impairment of immune function and the associated increased risk of infection."

Any time we read something like this, we get both excited and wary. The human body doesn't function via one simple ingredient, but by an unfathomable myriad of chemical reactions and environmental factors. Of the literature we've read recently, however, this study was the most conclusive in its support of a supplement. You be the judge.

⚠ **HMB** Beta-hydroxy-beta-methylbutyrate is a close chemical relative of the BCAA, leucine. Studies show that HMB benefits an endurance athlete's ability to maintain lean muscle mass during a period of high volume training combined with a strength-training phase.

At this time, there are no reported negative side-effects (besides being very expensive). The recommended dosage is 1.5 grams taken twice a day.

You can find HMB in supplement form, but make sure the label reads beta-hydroxy-beta-methylbutyrate in its exact spelling. There are a lot of pretenders out there. It's currently licensed to EAS (Experimental and Applied Sciences) via their parent company Metabolic Technologies, Inc.

⚠ **Medium Chain Triglycerides (MCTs)** These artificially developed fats aren't easily stored as body fat but have been shown to absorb quickly in the digestive tract, sparing glycogen during long endurance efforts. Taken in combination with your normal carbohydrate fuelling mixture, MCTs have proved to be a valuable energy source for endurance athletes in events of three hours or more.

There are no known negative side-effects. They can be found alone in liquid or capsule form as well as in a variety of nutritional supplements. For best results, mix the liquid form in with your fluid replacement drink or nutritional "shake" according to the label's instructions.

▲ **Phosphate**   Phosphate, in particular, sodium phosphate is a chemical compound proven to buffer lactic acid in athletes working at both sub-maximal and maximal intensities. This enables you to work at a higher level of intensity for a longer period of time. Translation? Improved performance in endurance activities. The longer the event gets (and the lower the intensity), the less of a positive effect phosphate will have (you don't need as much buffering at lower/more aerobic intensities).

Recommended dosage is a loading period that includes four grams a day for three days prior to an event. It is recommended that a lower dosage (1 to 2 grams / day) be administered for two to three days prior to the start of the loading period (in order to get your digestive system used to the phosphate). There is no "during event" dosage recommendation.

Possible negative side-effects can include gastrointestinal distress (especially if taken on an empty stomach) and long-term use can lead to problems with calcium absorption. Don't do more than three or four phosphate loading periods over the course of a year, or you're likely to face calcium absorption problems.

Phosphate can be found over the counter in health food stores; one example is Twin Lab's "Phos-Fuel".

▲ **Pyruvate**   Pyruvate is the main precursor in the production of ATP, which is the primary source of energy for muscular contraction. Studies have shown that oral supplementation in dosages of 3 to 5 grams per day can improve glucose absorption by muscle cells, improve levels of perceived effort and may act as an effective anti-oxidant.

Negative side-effects are limited to flatulence and cost. Pyruvate is found in supplemental form (capsules) on the retail shelf.

Questionable Performance Enhancers

There are other supplements we take or have taken during extremely hard training/racing. We feel the following examples were useful, so we've included our understanding of their purpose. Keep in mind that there isn't always research to back any of the claims made for many of these substances.

▲ **Carnitine/CoQ10 Supplement** These are taken in the morning, with or without your first meal/snack. Most products of this type provide approximately 1,500 mg of L-carnitine, 100 mg of Coenzyme Q10, 1,000 mg of Inosine monophosphate and some sodium and phosphorus.

Our understanding is that this combination helps increase lean body mass and regulate blood sugar, thereby improving performance. Keep in mind, we were taking this stuff back before clipless pedals…

▲ **Arginine/Lysine Supplements** Taken on an empty stomach (usually early morning), these provide L-arginine, L-lysine and Chromium Picolinate or an arginine/ornithine combination. The theory is that this combination stimulates production and release of human growth hormone (HGH). This helps build muscle and repair damage due to high training levels.

Keep in mind that a recent report flatly stated that there is no basis for the current claims regarding Chromium Picolinate as a "fat burner" or enhancer of muscle function.

▲ **Others** Other substances that are thought to improve performance include steroids (illegal and with a host of negative side-effects), herbal preparations (many are illegal and most have negative side-effects, particularly Ma Huang and ephedra), EPO (erythropoietin, illegal and with extremely negative side effects —

like death) and others too numerous to list. Most of these are taboo to any sport.

Chucky V (Velyupeck) told us about an incident that inspired him to get out of competitive cycling. A member of the U.S. national cycling team, he was competing in a prestigious amateur stage race in Italy. During one particularly hard stage, he saw a rider directly in front of him placing an amphetamine suppository during the final hour of the stage. As he said, "Here I am, racing my head off, about to be taken down by some joker in front of me descending at 50 mph with his finger up his butt!"

Shortly afterward, Velyupeck made the switch to triathlon.

Be Sensible

Having had the privilege of living and training with some of the best athletes in triathlon, we firmly believe that your best bet is a varied and moderate diet of good food, a sensible supplementation plan and a lot of hard work. There is no question that what you put into your body has a great effect on your health and performance. Like anything else, however, focusing too hard on nutrition can take away from the essence of what it takes to improve your performance: smart, sport-specific training.

CHAPTER 9
Mental Focus

Most people would agree with the statement, "If your mind is not calm and focused, you will not perform up to your potential." While we don't think that you can simply visualize your way to winning or even completing an event, we do think that you should tap certain elements of the mental side of training and racing.

Consider the amount of research and effort that is put into the physical side of sport, and how little is put into the mental aspect of sport. It's apparent (to us at least) that the power of the mind and the dormant possibilities that may exist there hold vast potential for improvement.

Two of the most common areas of concern are anxiety (usually due to expectations) and fear (either of pain or the unknown).

Anxiety can be put into proper perspective with the realization that you're the only one who really cares how you do in your event. Stop for a moment and ask yourself when was the last time you took note of anybody else's results. Chances are, you are familiar, in a general sense, with where some people have finished in various races, yet you probably have this overwhelming sense that others out there actually know how you did and have attached some judgment to your performance.

The reality is quite different.

Expectations can only have two possible outcomes. They are either met or missed. There is either success or failure. Why not leave both personal and external expectations behind and, instead, simply give the best effort you can under the conditions the day presents? If you are able to do that, you have had a successful day — no matter what the clock says.

Fear of the unknown should not factor into the race experience at all. If you've been training consistently, you pretty much know what will happen on race day. It is a mistake to expect something spectacularly different during your event. Yet some people expect the heavens will part and they will be propelled to the finish line without having to breathe hard or feel any burning in their legs.

Training is the opportunity to experience the realities that racing presents. Manage your anxiety and fear by taking care of what is in your "power":

- Train intelligently
- Make sure your equipment is in order
- Know the course
- Dress for the weather conditions
- Pace yourself
- Know exactly where your bike is racked in the transition area

Put Bodyglide on seams that might chafe you.

There are numerous practical details that can keep your mind focused and occupied away from the issues over which you have no control – the weather, the water temperature, the wind and how well someone else has prepared. Remember, you have worked hard – this is all about you!

Helpful Hints for Having a Successful Race Day

Racing in various venues (often big cities) brings with it some unique technicalities. Being prepared is important in order to have as smooth a weekend as possible.

A big city race can have a lot of traffic issues. For that reason it is not really advisable to get out on your bike on the roads the day before the race. Use a turbo trainer or a lifecycle if possible – or skip the ride altogether. There is no need to take unnecessary risks. If you really need to check if your gears are working, find a quiet parking lot to test them out.

Try to get your race check-in during off-peak hours, so you can minimize the time you spend standing in line.

Make sure your USA Triathlon license is current before you get to the event. If you are not signed up as an annual member, you may do so at www.usatriathlon.org. Otherwise, you may have to purchase a single event license for $7 at race check-in.

Try to get your bearings in the day(s) before the event so that you are clear on where you will be going on race morning, understand where to park and know how to get to the start and from the finish line to your car/home/hotel/friends.

At a large event, the number of bikes in the transition area is very large. Make sure that you are very clear about where your bike is racked. Count how many rows back you are, or tie a balloon on the rack where your bike is located. After the effort of the swim and the run to the transition area, things can get very confusing.

It is a good idea to have your tires pumped before you leave home/hotel, as it minimizes the stuff you have to take with you.

Get down to the transition area at least ONE HOUR prior to the start of your wave, or whenever the race organization has stipulated. If there are a lot of wave starts, make sure you are very clear when you particular wave is scheduled to start.

Make sure that you are correctly body-marked so there is less possibility of timing mix-ups, and you can get accurate results.

Leave the transition area in plenty of time to get down to the swim start and to get your wetsuit on in time.

Take some extra toilet tissue down with you, in case they run out at the public rest rooms or port-a-johns.

Take extra fluids and a snack (energy bar) with you, in case of unexpected delays. Other essentials are sunscreen and Bodyglide (or other lubricant) to put on where seams in your wetsuit may cause chafing. This is especially important in the neck area of your wetsuit.

Do at least a small warm-up in the morning to get yourself moving and calm pre-race nerves. A nice 5-10 minute jog is fine; and if possible jump into the water for a minute or two before your wave goes off.

Read all the race literature carefully, including the rules. That way you will not be caught by surprise, and you will be on time and prepared. This, along with your precise plan, should maximize the potential for a great day.

This is what you should be visualizing before – and at all the tough spots during – your race. Triathlon is a mental game. There's nothing more effective than positive thinking.

CHAPTER 10
Race Day

Before you do your first triathlon, you probably have no idea what to expect or what to do in the transition areas. While it's only natural to be a little nervous, take heart! Everything will be relatively simple, though you might not know it from this long explanation.

Get to the race at least one hour before your wave is scheduled to start. Get to know the flow of transition with a quick reconnaissance — where does the swim enter, where does the bike exit, where does the bike enter, where does the run exit, where does the run finish?

Get numbered, find your bike rack/transition space, and get set up. Rack your bike and lay a towel on the ground. Put your cycling shoes (unbuckled or unlaced) toward the front of the towel

— closest to you — and your running shoes toward the back of the towel (toward the rack) with your hat, singlet, etc. You can put your helmet on your bike with the buckle undone and glasses in the helmet ready to put on.

If it's a short race, take your bike out and ride for 15 minutes or so to warm your legs up. Rack the bike and go for a 5 to 10 minute jog. Come back and, with 20 to 25 minutes to go before your start time, put your wetsuit on (if you're wearing one) and get to the swim start no later than 15 minutes prior to the start.

Seed yourself according to your swimming ability. If you're really fast, go ahead and get on the front line. If not, get to the outside of the group, where you can be sure to have some clear water to swim in if you get crowded from one side. If you're on the same side as the buoy line coming into a turn, you might get a lot of congestion into the turn as athletes outside of you try to cut the turn as sharply as possible — so it's best to be on the outside.

If you're wearing a wetsuit, wear what you intend to wear for the entire race under that wetsuit (including running/cycling shorts, a singlet and race numbers) — it saves on transition time spent changing.

When you enter transition from the swim, you should have already pulled your zipper open and gotten your wetsuit to waist level. When you get to your bike, pull the wetsuit down to your knees and step out of it. High step to get the wetsuit off your legs, putting your helmet and sunglasses on at the same time. This isn't easy, so either practice it at home until you get it down, or slow down your transition and do things one at a time.

Next, put your bike shoes on and run your bike to the bike exit. Mount your bike and you're off.

Practice taking your feet out of your shoes while still on the bike and stepping on top of them. This allows you to keep pedalling until the last minute as you enter the bike transition. Dismount where you're told to and run your bike to your rack.

Don't ever unbuckle your helmet until both feet are on the ground! This is one of the fastest ways to be disqualified.

Note: it's important that your cranks are at 3 and 9 o'clock so your shoes don't get knocked off the pedals. They'll usually naturally find this position on their own, but keep an eye on them when you begin to run with the bike to make sure they arrive at this position. Better yet, quickly give them a turn to the appropriate position.

When you get to your spot, rack your bike, take off your helmet and sunglasses and you're off to the run exit.

Know where your transition is by counting the racks as you come from the swim to bike entrance and from the bike to run entrance, or note a landmark close to your bike. The transition area doesn't look the same during the chaos of the race and all the bikes and gear look very much the same.

Go through the act of a transition in practice. Get it down in your head so that there's a logical sequence to your transition. Don't rush. Be smooth and methodical.

Lace locks on your running shoes can save a lot of time and anguish — you can even try elastic laces that allow you to slip your shoes on without any additional hassle.

Do NOT try anything new on race day! That goes for equipment, nutrition, etc. Try new things in training.

Going through an Aid Station is like going through
a carwash. Have a plan before you get there.
Don't rush! Slow down & eat your gel when you see
the aid station in the distance, then grab a drink,
grab a sponge, grab a shower and get going.

CHAPTER 12
Resources

Cycling

Bicycle Federation of America, 1506 21st St #200 NW, Washington DC 20036, 202/463-6622

IMBA, Post Office Box 7578, Boulder, CO 80306, 303/545-9011

International Mountain Biking Assn, nonprofit group that promotes mountain biking, PO Box 7578, Boulder, CO 80306, 303/545-9011, Imba@aol.com, www.imba.com

League of American Bicyclists, national membership organization, 1612 K Street NW, Ste. 401, Washington DC, 20006, 202/822-1333, www.bikeleague.org

United States Cycling Federation, governing body for amateur cycling, One Olympic Plaza, Colorado Springs, CO 80909-5775, 719/578-4581

United States Professional Cycling Federation, governing body for professional cycling, One Olympic Plaza, Colorado Springs, CO 80909, 719/578-4581

Running/Track & Field

American Running & Fitness Assn, not-for-profit organization to educate runners and other fitness enthusiasts, 4405 E/W Highway #405, Bethesda, MD 20814, 800-776-2732, www.arfa.org

Road Runners Club of America (RRCA), national association of running clubs, 1150 S. Washington Street #250, Alexandria, VA 22314, 703/836-0558, e-mail office@rrca.org, website www.rrca.org

USA Track & Field, national governing body for road racing, cross-country, track & field & race walking events, PO Box 120, Indianapolis, IN 46206, 317/261-0500

Swimming

Aquatic Exercise Assn, resource center for aquatic fitness (vertical exercise in the pool), PO Box 1609, Nokomis, FL 34274, 941/486-8600, www.aeawave.com

U.S. Swimming, One Olympic Plaza, Colorado Springs, CO 80809, 719/578-4578

Triathlon

USA Triathlon Federation, 3595 E. Fountain Blvd. #F-1, Colorado Springs, CO 80910, 719/597-9090, membership services, 800-874-1872

World Triathlon Corporation, Ironman Mainland Office, PO Box 1608, Tarpon Springs, FL 34688, 813/942-4767, www.ironmanlive.com

Hot Links

www.active.com
Nationwide source for thousands of participatory sports events.

www.fitnesszone.com
Shop fitnesszone.com for bikes, free-weights, aerobic supplies, etc. Obtain free fitness profiles, online fitness articles, gym locator (locate any gym in the U.S.). Fitness forums, classifieds, fitness library.

www.runnersworld.com
Training tips, recent issue articles, nutrition tips, travel, statistics, shoes, awards, forums, injury prevention tips and descriptions.

www.sports-medicine.com
Preventing injuries, search for your injury, ask Dr. Zeman, exercise, accidents and legal medicine, career links in sports medicine.

www.acefitness.org
American Council on Exercise. Fit facts, news releases, find a certified professional.

www.insidetri.com
Find a triathlon.

www.multisports.com
Current news, events and archives on multi-sports.

www.triathletemag.com
Current news and archives on the sport of triathlon.

www.competitor.com
Current news, events and archives on multi-sports in Southern California.

www.citysportsmag.com
Current news, events and archives on multi-sports in Northern California.

www.floridasports.com
Current news, events and archives on multi-sports in Florida.

www.citysportsnw.com
Current news, events and archives on multi-sports in the Pacific Northwest.

www.eatright.org/find.html
Find a nutritionist near you.

www.endureplus.com/coaching.cfm
Find a coach on the Internet.

ABOUT THE AUTHORS

Paul Huddle Endurance Multi Sport Coach

During his twelve-year career as a professional triathlete, Paul Huddle finished over twenty Ironman distance events (nine in Hawaii) and well over 300 triathlons. He was top-ten finisher at Ironman Triathlon World Championship in Kona, Hawaii in 1990, '92 and '93; with a best time of 8:27:24. He won Ironman Japan ('91); the International Strongman Triathlon ('91, '93); the Ironhorse Triathlon; and the Wildflower Triathlon (1989 & 1991). He also had top-five finishes at Ironman Lanzarote, New Zealand, Canada and Japan.

As a partner in Multisports.com, Huddle is involved in production, administration and instruction at triathlon camps and clinics all over the world. Multisports.com produces annual adult camps and offers on-line coaching for swimming, running, cycling and triathlon for athletes of all levels of ability. Huddle co-writes the popular column, "Dear Coach" for *Triathlete Magazine* and personally coaches Paula Newby-Fraser, Chris Legh, Spencer Smith and several age group champions at both the Ironman and Olympic distances.

With a B.S. in Food Science from the University of Arizona at Tucson, he is a member of USA Triathlon's Coaching Advisory Board for the design and implementation of athlete and coaching competency requirements and was certified as a Sport, Expert and Elite level coach by USA Cycling at the Olympic Training Center in Colorado Springs, CO. He has also been certified by the American Council on Exercise (ACE) as a Personal Trainer.

Roch Frey Endurance Multi Sport Coach

A former professional triathlete from Canada, Roch Frey has been involved with triathlon for over twenty years. After winning the Canadian Long Course National Championships in 1993, he turned to full-time coaching and founded the UCSD Master's Triathlon Training Club. He built a triathlon training program in San Diego's north county and works with 15-20 triathletes each year on a one-to-one basis, including Heather Fuhr, 1997 Ironman Hawaii Champion and Peter Reid, 1998 and 2000 Ironman Hawaii Champion.

In 1999, Frey combined forces with Paul Huddle, Paula Newby-Fraser and John Duke to create Multisports.com. They hold triathlon-training camps throughout the world. In addition, he and Paul Huddle established online training programs that cover all distances of triathlons from sprint to Ironman and accommodate all levels of triathletes.

In 2000, Frey took his coaching expertise to the sport of Adventure Racing. He and Huddle were the head coaches for the Asian MSOQ Team, spending several weeks in China preparing the team for this four-day stage event. With Huddle, he writes *Triathlete Magazine's* "Dear Coach" column, and serves as race and course director for a variety of events.

Frey has a B.S. in Physical Education, Coaching/Exercise Physiology from the University of Alberta. A graduate of the National Coaching Certification Program (NCCP) in Canada, he holds certificates in Level 3 Theory, Level 3 Technical, Triathlon Level 2 Technical, Swimming, Cycling, Running and Level 1 Paddling Instructor. He is a member of the American Swim Coaches Association, USA Triathlon and Triathlon Canada.

Bob Babbitt Multi Sport Publisher

A publisher, writer and editor for fitness-related magazines for sixteen years, Bob Babbitt has co-written or ghost-written several fitness-related books, including *Mark Allen's Total Triathlete, Biathlon Training and Racing Techniques,* and *Workouts for Working People* with Mark Allen and Julie Moss. His offbeat, personal style appeals to athletes and non-athletes alike.

Babbitt co-owns fitness publications in Florida, California, Washington and Oregon. He also hosts a weekly radio show on 77,000 watt superstation XTRA Sports 690 in Southern California. His television on-air credits include the Ironkids Triathlon Championships on ESPN; Ironman Lanzarote, Ironman Canada and Ironman Germany on ESPN; The Xtreme Golf World Championships on ESPN; and the San Diego Marathon on Fox Sports. He has been an active promoter, chronicler, participant and fan of triathlon since the earliest days of the sport.

A six-time finisher of the Ironman Triathlon, Babbitt has completed twenty-five marathons and was recently named the tenth inductee into the Ironman Triathlon Hall of Fame.